The Simple World

Daniel Ostermayer

Richard Feinburg, a mathematician and computer scientist famous for his educational videos and public musings on civilization, has retired to a small San Diego beach community. A month earlier, Walter Carlisle and his wife Chloe had moved to the neighborhood as they prepared to start a family. Leaving for work, Walter noticed Richard unpacking a few boxes on the porch of the bungalow next door. Starstruck, he worked up the courage to introduce himself.

Introductions

Walter: Good morning.

Richard: Hi young lad.

Walter: Are you Richard Feinburg?

Richard: Of course, who else would I be?

Walter: Wow, it's a pleasure to meet you. Welcome to the neighborhood. I'm Walter. I live next door.

Richard: Nice to meet you Walter. Is it just you next door?

Walter: Just me and my wife. Although we're expecting our first child in a few months. We're new here as well. Just moved in a month ago.

Richard: Congratulations, that's wonderful. I'll keep a lookout for the baby balloons. And what's your wife's name if you don't mind me asking?

Walter: Chloe

Richard: Are you two expecting a son or a daughter?

Walter: Still a mystery. We've decided to be surprised.

Richard: That's exciting. Nothing like a little old fashioned surprise.

Walter: By the way, your last book was fantastic. It's one of the few books I've ever read twice.

Richard: Glad you liked it. I'm still surprised by its popularity. The history of the universe and modern times isn't traditionally best seller material.

Walter: You're being modest. That book was eye opening. It'll be tough for you to go unrecognized here, even in a sleepy beach neighborhood.

Richard: I guess so, but you're the only person to say hello in over a week. It's nice to go unnoticed but I feel a little weird, especially coming from Boulder, where everyone knew me.

Walter: Oh really? Have you met the Shah's? Faraz and Dahlia live two houses down. They have two little kids always playing outside.

Richard: Oh yes, I have waved and said hello, but never got much more than a curious stare. People seem to be initially distrusting of new neighbors. You never know, I could be a criminal.

Walter: Ha! Don't take it personally. Sometimes people are just too busy to make an introduction.

Richard: What do you do for work if you don't mind me asking?

Walter: Software engineer at a local startup. Our offices are just down the hill. We work out of the corporate center in the big modern building next to Sandra's Coffee. You walk right by it on the way to the beach.

Richard: Yes, I think I know which one you're talking about. I always stop and get coffee at Sandra's. What's the company name? I never paid attention to the sign out front.

Walter: It's called Giga. We make distributive hosting software so you can earn money from your unused hard drive space and computing power. Essentially you host other people's content and get micropayments in exchange.

Richard: I haven't heard of it but the concept sounds similar to IPFS where you store other peoples files but can't access them.

Walter: Yes exactly. When the company started we were planning on rolling out our product on top of the InterPlanetary File System but from what I gather the founders had some issues with the IPFS developers.

Richard: That's really fascinating. Well, it's a pleasure to meet you. You look like you're headed to work so don't let me keep you.

Water: Yes. I'm actually a few minutes late so I'd better get going. Talk to you later

Richard: Yes sir.

A week after Richard moved in, a little shipping container was dropped off outside of his house. It overhung the driveway a small amount so anyone walking past on the sidewalk needed to go into the street to get past. Slowly he unpacked it. On a few occasions, Walter offered to help, but Richard always declined. He seemed content to slowly bring a box or two out per day. Curiously, there were never movers to help with furniture and the pod was far to small for a house full of things.

The Phone

Walter: Good morning Richard. How was the surf?

Richard: Nice and small. I'm still learning but I always have so much fun. I stood up for the first time yesterday. Pretty good for a man about to turn 70.

Walter: Not bad at all. I've only tried surfing a few times and could never stay on the board. Hey, I realized I never gave you my phone number. Just in case you ever need anything you should have it.

Richard: Hold on, let me get my phone. It's inside.

Sorry for taking so long I couldn't find it and it's probably without charge. Here, I wrote my number down, just send me a message and I'll get it when I find my phone.

Walter: I guess being off the grid is becoming pretty trendy.

Richard: I'm hardly a trend setter. I'm more accidentally off grid. I don't purposefully ignore my phone, but I rarely carry it anywhere so I tend to lose it. I'm sure I'll find it eventually.

Walter: Don't you worry about missing an important call?

Richard: Not really. And if someone needs my immediate assistance, talking to me by phone won't help.

Walter: That's not true. What if a friend needs to get it touch for an emergency. Doesn't that worry you?

Richard: No not really. I know it sounds selfish but even though people might feel the need to tell me they need help, and I might feel the need to know that they need help, if I'm not in a position to help, nothing can be done by contacting me by phone.

Umm…say a friend calls me and tells me that they are in the hospital. That call doesn't help their condition. And I would have found out anyway when I get their message later. I'm not a doctor so I really can't help even though it is nice to know and provide them with some emotional support.

Knowing right away is often not as important as it seems. It isn't that I don't want to get their call, it's that I don't need their call or the information immediately. I always make sure my voicemail has space. And besides, they can send off a mass text message which includes me and many other people to maximize the chances of reaching someone.

Walter: OK, I guess so.

Richard: I want to know about things that I can act on. If I can't act, knowing is fine but usually not that important.

Let's take it one step further. Say a friend calls and needs to get picked up because her car broke down a few miles away. She should really just call a cab or a tow truck. Calling me is fine and I will answer if I'm available but if I don't answer it means I can't help at that moment.

I had an old college friend who got arrested for disorderly conduct at a bar and called me from the police station. I was busy preparing a lecture so I didn't answer my phone.

The next morning, I returned his call and helped pick him up when he was released.

Walter: Please don't take this the wrong way, but do people get annoyed with your approach to being conveniently unavailable?

Richard: Yes of course. I've been accused of being selfish by many friends who wanted to get in touch with me immediately but had to wait until I call back. I still help out whenever I can but just do so on an alternative schedule.

Walter: I get what you're saying. If I were to do that I'd feel terribly guilty.

Richard: Many years ago a friend who was a psychologist asked me during a joint family vacation if it was better to be selfish or selfless. My first reaction was exactly in line with what you're saying, "Of course it's better to be selfless".

But, my friend countered my answer with a story of a famous physician who had the option to go away and study at a prestigious school while his mother was very sick or stay at home and wait for her to die from a terminal disease. The doctor chose to go away, learn his craft, and cure thousands of people as a famous oncologic surgeon. For awhile his siblings hated him and accused him of abandoning his family in a time of need. They claimed he chose his own goals over the needs of his family.

But, his mother never died. She recovered against all odds. Did he make the right choice by being selfish and heading off to school knowing his mother might die without him at her side?

Walter: Well he wasn't exactly being selfish if his goal was to learn a skill that would help so many people.

Richard: Well, his family certainly thought he was selfish.

Walter: Right, but he was trying to do something good for others by being a doctor. That's a pretty selfless profession.

Richard: What he did in the operating room gave him constant happiness. Doctors have a lot of personal satisfaction from their work.

Walter: Enjoying your work doesn't make you selfish.

Richard: Pursuing happiness is selfish. I think you're pushing back on this because like most people, you see selfishness as inherently bad. It's not. Selfishness propels us to do great things.

Even the most wonderful and seemingly selfless acts contain small drops of selfishness. A rich CEO donates millions of dollars anonymously to a wonderful cause. This seems like an incredible display of altruism with no external recognition. But the donor experiences some internal satisfaction and contentment with the choice. Internal self-gratification powers most acts of generosity.

Selfishness extends all the way down to our DNA. We don't reproduce for the good of humanity. We have children for ourselves because without a new generation our own genes would vanish from the planet. Sex is pleasurable for a reason. Many things are selfish, but I can't think of one thing that's selfless.

Walter: Not sure I can disagree but it's still quite a stretch to relate this small level of inherent selfishness to not carrying a phone.

Richard: It's simply a spectrum. Sometimes I'm very selfish and other times less so. I carry the phone when I know that I can be available to help and I don't carry it when I'm unavailable. Better for a friend to reach me when I'm able to be of assistance than to waste time talking to me when I really cannot help.

Walter: OK, sorry for coming off so intense about your lost phone. I really didn't mean to accuse you of doing something wrong.

Richard: Oh it's totally OK. It's fun to have an intense discussion every once in a while.

Walter: Sorry again. I'll see you later.

For Yourself not Others

Richard: Good morning Walter. Good news, I found my phone! Turns out I never even unpacked it. And I found a few old hard drives I needed as well.

Walter: Lots of missed calls? What's it been, a month since you moved in?

Richard: Yeah, about a month. Surprisingly only a few calls. Let me send you a text. I finally added your phone number. Did you get it?

Walter: Yep, just got it.

Richard: I was thinking about our conversation regarding taking time without a phone. I feel like I made it into a larger philosophical point than it needed to be. It really just boils down to being present in the moment. With the phone on and in my pocket, I can be interrupted anywhere, anytime, for any reason. I just can't be present and focused if that type of interruption can occur. The phone makes every moment like living on a busy street and leaving your doors and windows open. Anything or anyone can come in without warning.

Walter: I completely understand the need to be focused and uninterrupted. I didn't mean to be so confrontational about it. My apologies. I totally agree with you about staying focused. Especially during family time, the phone is a massive distraction.

Richard: Yes, I find it also helps to not have a phone when traveling.

Walter: That would be a tough sell. Having an instantly updated universal map in your pocket when lost is priceless.

Richard: Of course, but you can always ask someone for help. I know it seems old fashioned but people are very willing to give directions, and paper maps don't require charging.

More importantly, traveling without a phone really means traveling without a camera. Since the phone is really my camera I'm forced to try and remember what I see without the ability to take a photo. And also without the ability to share the photo.

I like being free from the temptation to post a photo and then check the comments. No phone means traveling without the the justification of others. It affords an incredible sense of freedom that I once had before the era of ubiquitous smartphones.

Walter: I never thought about it that way. Traveling without the justification of others is an interesting way of thinking about avoiding social media.

Richard: Why travel if the enjoyment comes from the likes generated by the photos you post? Why travel if you could be interrupted at any time? I couldn't answer any of these questions, so I stopped bringing my phone when exploring a new place. I just leave it in the hotel. Now I travel because I want to, not because I want to tell people I'm traveling.

Walter: That's certainly extreme. It sounds wonderful, but I think there's definitely a middle ground of only sharing with friends and family.

Richard: Yes of course. Moderation is often right, but sometimes abstinence is best.

After a few days of pestering, Richard finally convinced Walter to come surfing on a clear Saturday morning. He loaned Walter a board and wetsuit and they met on the sidewalk at 6am for a walk down to the beach. The morning breeze carried a cool mist that disappeared as they arrived at the shore. For the first hour Richard gave a few pointers and then they just paddled around missing most waves until finally catching one and riding it all the way to shore. With big smiles on their faces, they paddled back out and then coasted back to shore with the rising tide.

The Self

Walter: Nice catch on that last wave. You really looked good.

Richard: Yeah, it just felt right when I paddled into it. If I had known surfing was so much fun I would have moved to the beach years ago.

Walter: Yes it's certainly a lifestyle that I could get used to as well. Not sure I have the time to do it everyday but I bet my arms are gong to be really sore tomorrow.

Richard: Yeah, your shoulders are going to feel like jelly.

Walter: Sorry to keep bringing this up, but I'm still not sure you're right on your theory of selfishness. I can't stop thinking about what we've been talking about. You claim everyone is selfish but I've heard you say in interviews that you pride yourself on fighting against the "sense of self". How do you square these two philosophies? It seems like a contradiction.

Richard: People are selfish because we get pleasure from doing good things. We can't suppress the dopamine regardless of how stoic we try to be. Our body wants to feel good. Selfishness is programmed into our biology. Whenever we do something good, our brain experiences positive feedback that encourages the selfish behavior. Even people who claim to do something solely for the good of someone else, get stimulus from their pleasure pathway.

When I talk about the non-self I'm saying, "No man is an island". People are not fully independent, and never self-sufficient. In other words there is no self without others.

Walter: OK this is where I'm still confused. If there is no self, how can people be inherently selfish?

Richard: The non-self is is different from selfishness. The non-self refers to our identity, while selfishness refers to our desires.

When I say that I'm cultivating the non-self, I'm referring to the fact that my identity, my desires, my every fiber, even my biology, is an amalgamation of every experience in my life. I try to cultivate an awareness of my unimportance. The non-self is the culmination of this reasoning. It's the conscious acknowledgement that we're nothing more than the sum of our experiences interacting with the sum of our internal biology.

Walter: So we think we're self-sufficient individuals but we're really just a product of our environment. Is this right?

Richard: Yes, exactly! We act selfishly because we still have desires, goals, and wants, but each of us is a combination of everything in our lives. Our desires only exist because of the current environment and past experiences. Therefore our self is really a non-self. Maybe we should call it something else like a "combo person" but we're stuck with the term self. So non-self is just the opposite.

We're literally nothing without our family and friends. We would think differently if raised in a different country or time period. We would probably have a different job if raised by different parents in a different economic situation. Our diet influences our biology. Our body responds to how much we exercise, sleep, and eat, and that response is unpredictable. Much of our existence is dependent on mysterious chemical balances and imbalances.

Walter: So in your eyes, selfishness is really just another way of saying satisfying our own interest. But this has nothing to do with our identity.

Richard: Yes. We have our own interests. And we certainly get happiness from our personal decisions. That's fundamentally true.

Walter: But those individual desires and interests are influenced by factors mainly outside our control?

Richard: Yes. When taken in that context, it reveals that we are really a thing made of and dependent on many other things. This make the self a myth. The self is really a non-self.

Imagine living in medieval England, you would never identify as a computer programmer. Your occupation would be entirely dependent on the time of your existence.

Now, imagine you were forced to fight in a war for one year in the current time period. You would have a very different outlook on life after that stressful year. You would still be the same physical person but your identity and thought process would have changed. The environment changes us. We adapt our identity to our surroundings. This is the non-self. It is the acknowledgment that humans are a product of time and space.

Walter: I think you've convinced me. That makes sense. We do things because of our desires, but our desires are really not fully ours. They're shaped by many factors outside of our control.

Richard: Yes. And as soon as you let go of your personal identity, you begin to relax your expectations of what should and should not occur. Thinking about myself as really nothing more than a collection of interactions with others and my internal cellular arrangement, has made me exceedingly happy.

Walter: And if it didn't make you happy would you have ever made such a big deal about the non-self in the first place?

Richard: Of course not. But that doesn't make it more or less true.

While walking home from the beach after a late morning surf session by himself, Richard noticed the struggles of a postal worker attempting to move a box that looked the size of a dresser. He always had empathy for those working such thankless jobs delivering the mail, so he helped him bring the box onto Walter's porch. Since everyone was at work, he left a note saying he'd be back at night to help bring the box inside. When he returned, three more massive boxes were blocking the Carlisles' front steps.

Being Light

Walter: Thanks for bringing this up from the sidewalk today.

Richard: Happy to help. The waves were a bit choppy so I didn't spend much time at the beach. I bumped into the postman on the way up the hill.

Walter: Oh yeah. There's a storm coming in from Mexico.

Richard: May I offer a few words of advice?

Walter: Of course.

Richard: Your life is going to start getting heavy. Keep an eye out for opportunities to stay light.

Walter: What do you mean? The new responsibilities of being a parent?

Richard: Yes that's unavoidable. What I mean, is all the stuff you are going to be tempted to buy for your child and yourself. You'll buy stuff with the intent of saving time but will paradoxically lose time in the process.

Walter: I know. I think we already have too much stuff. If that wasn't glaringly obvious. Lots of gifts from family.

By the way, this is going to sound like a silly question but I've been meaning to ask you. I hope this isn't too personal, but do you have any furniture?

Richard: Funny you ask. I have a small cot as a bed right now. Other than that I haven't felt the need to buy anything yet.

Walter: You've been here for a few months and still live in an empty house?

Richard: Yes, it's been nice. I'm starting over and taking my time deciding on the appropriate level of clutter.

Walter: And you didn't travel out here with anything but that pod in your driveway?

Richard: When I sold my house in Boulder I included all the furniture for the new owner. I just moved with this little shipping pod and have essentially been camping in my house. I like to stay as light as possible. Have you weighted your life?

Walter: I'm 180 pounds, about 20 pounds overweight.

Richard: Very funny. You know what I mean, how light are you?

Walter: Not light at all. After only three months of living in this house, we have way too much stuff.

Richard: See, it's easy to be full and hard to stay empty. How easy and quickly could you move to a new place? Each year I look for ways to make myself lighter.

Walter: And you donate unnecessary stuff each year?

Richard: Initially donating is the way to go. Take an inventory of everything you own and think about its necessity. Then ask, "If I were fleeing the country, would I take this?"

Walter: OK that seems a little extreme. I'm all for minimalism but at some point you need stuff. And if you were fleeing no matter how minimal your life, a lot of your things would be left behind.

Richard: Yes of course it's an extreme example. But I purposefully use it because only extreme situations cause quick and decisive action. Only when surprised do we learn. Only when shocked with a radical idea do we change our mind.

So I ask myself this crazy question about fleeing the country. What I get in return are great solutions for lightening my life.

Walter: Do you ever decide to make life heavier?

Richard: Of course. I buy things but I get them because I really need them, not because I want to fill up space. I keep my time preference low and flexibility high.

Walter: Time preference?

Richard: Yes, it's a measure of immediate vs delayed gratification. Do you value an instantly full house knowing you probably didn't think everything through and will change your mind just as quickly? Or do you value a slow accumulation of wealth and high quality property? High time preferences is instant, low time preference is long term. It's a term from economics, sometimes referred to as time-discounting.

Walter: Interesting. I never heard of it, but I get it. Being light is easier said than done, especially with children. I'm jealous of your simplicity.

Richard: Don't be. Anyone can do it, but for some reason the default is always more not less. I like possessions just like everyone else, but too much stuff weighs down the mind. Accumulation is like mental obesity.

Walter: How so?

Richard: Well, I used to play bass guitar but when I was consulting on the particle accelerator at CERN and our family was living in France, I would go to work, come home, play with the kids, and then stay up late debugging code written the day before. The guitar sitting next to my desk was always calling my name to play. I felt guilty since I couldn't find time to practice.

This feeling of guilt made me very volatile. I'd snap at my wife Janice and complain about being overworked. Finally, I realized that it wasn't that I was overworked, it was that I felt drawn to do other less important things like play guitar. If I didn't have those things then I wouldn't feel stressed. The bass became a burden and I realized it didn't fit into my life and maybe wouldn't fit in for years.

One day I sold it to a friend who played it all the time. I felt mentally free, focused, and happy. Without the distraction I could live more in the present and do what fit into the time I had available. Playing with kids, and working became the only things I had time for and the only things I really wanted to do.

Walter: And you didn't feel a little bit empty without your guitar?

Richard: Quite the opposite. I felt more full because my attention was focused on the important things. I worked, hung out with my family, and had one less thing to spread my precious time amongst. This is what I mean by feeling light.

Walter: And later on, did you get a new bass?

Richard: No, I don't play anymore. But I now own a surfboard. Of course I loved making music but I have other toys that occupy my time. When you have too much stuff, maintenance and attention to the items become a chore.

I have countless friends who have lots of hobbies, boats, bikes, golf clubs, and are always frustrated that they don't have enough time for their hobbies, or lament the time and practice it takes to maintain their skills. I tell them, "lighten up." Sell off the extra stuff, reduce life to the essentials, and then gradually add back in a few activities and items. Instead of feeling pulled between so many things, focus on just one or two really important activities. It helps lessen the guilt you feel from having a dusty old motorcycle you never ride. Lightening up also helps you feel more free to pursue the things you want to do with the time you have available.

It also helps free your identity. Many people define themselves by their hobbies. They say, “I'm a golfer and a cyclist.” This makes change very hard because as soon as they stop doing one of those things, they're vexed.

Walter: Vexed?

Richard: Yes, distraught, weighted down by guilt, mentally troubled. Stuff makes us more heavy mentally than physically. It's as if we put an anchor down that takes enormous strength to raise and our boat is trapped out at sea. We never change course because we have no lightness of identity.

So I like to keep my identity as light as my name. I am not a writer, or a mathematician, or a programmer, or a public speaker. I am just Richard Feinburg and nothing else.

The following evening as Richard headed inside after spending a few hours stargazing, he noticed the Carlisles' garage door still open with a light on. Wondering if they had forgotten to close it, he walked over to check. Instead, he saw a frustrated Richard, surrounded by tools and cardboard boxes, struggling to build an unnecessarily complex dresser and crib. Clearly he needed help deciphering the convoluted instructions.

Children

Walter: I really appreciate your help. I'm sure you have something more important to do than build this monstrosity. This was inside those boxes you helped bring in yesterday.

Richard: Being semi-retired has its perks. Little in the way of evening obligations.

Walter: Well, thanks again.

Richard: How are you two doing? Nervous? Excited for your baby's birthday?

Walter: Probably more nervous than anything. How many kids do you have again?

Richard: I had two. But my wife and children died many years ago in a plane crash.

Walter: Oh my, I'm so sorry. I just assumed they were living elsewhere. And you mentioned them once before. Forgive me for even bringing up the subject.

Richard: It's OK. You would never have known. I never talked about it publicly. Their loss, as terrible as it was, taught me quite a lot about life. Times were very dark for a few years.

Walter: No really, we don't need to talk about this. Forget I even brought it up.

Richard: Unless it makes you uncomfortable, I like talking about them. I miss them everyday, but I had no control over their loss. And wishing that they were back changes nothing. Talking about them gives me the opportunity to refresh some great memories.

Walter: OK.

Richard: Could I tell you a story?

Walter: Sure, if you're offering.

Richard: Janice and I had James and Zoe four years apart. I was finishing some research at Livermore National Lab when our youngest was born. We were living in the Bay Area just as it started to get expensive.

My mentor at the time shared the best advice with me right before James was born. He said, "Always remember, your children owe you nothing. They didn't ask to exist. You created them and you owe them everything."

At the time I didn't really recognize the wisdom. Later on when things were getting even more expensive and I was stressed over them learning as much as they could in a not so great public school, I remembered his advice. It wasn't about them living up to my expectations of grades, interests and future accomplishments. I needed to live up to their expectations. I owed them the promise of providing an atmosphere so they could flourish in whatever way they wanted. We couldn't afford private school or moving to a different neighborhood, so, we moved out of the Bay Area to Boulder. This way they could grow up in the outdoors with great schooling, affordable living, and we could save money for their future.

Walter: Agreed. So many parents expect their children to live up to their goals or personal aspirations. Having no expectations is probably a very freeing and also loving way to raise kids. At the same time I can't imagine not having some hopes and dreams for them.

Richard: Have a framework with rules and desires that can adjust as you child grows. But at the same time don't forget, you asked for your child. Your child didn't ask for you.

Walter: Thanks again for the help. Would you want to come in for a drink?

Richard: No thanks, it's time for me to retire for the night. I'll take a raincheck.

Walter: 'Night Richard.

Slowly over the course of a year, Richard removed the various odds and ends from the moving pod that never seemed to leave the driveway. He took so long unpacking that he paid a fine to the city for leaving the container obstructing the sidewalk. The last few items were much too heavy for a 70-year-old man to lift, so he finally enlisted Walter's help.

Why work

Richard: Thanks for helping move this old storage crate. I know you're busy at home with your new baby. What's his name?

Walter: Cody

Richard: Nice. How's he doing?

Walter: Seems to be doing well. Never sleeping as you would expect.

Richard: Hang in there. It doesn't get much easier, even when kids finally decide to sleep.

Walter: Well that's good to know. What's in this box by the way? It's like a ton of bricks.

Richard: Lots of old books and manuscripts from my academic days.

Walter: Why did you leave academia? Especially after having spent time getting your PhD?

Richard: Why do you ask? Considering going back to school?

Walter: A long time ago, I considered enrolling in a PhD program but couldn't bring myself to go into more debt. I never saw the upside. I'm just curious, as I always admired your work, but if you never did public talks or TV shows, I would never have heard of you. It's your work outside of the university that inspired me.

Richard: Thanks for the compliment. I've often wondered why I got my PhD. Perhaps it was just sunk cost. The degree, however, did give me instant credibility regardless of whether it was deserved.

Walter: From what you've said in interviews you were working on some of the hardest data-structure problems in early computing as an undergrad. Certainly you could have worked for anyone right after your bachelors. I doubt you needed credibility. Plus you must have endured many years without a good salary.

Richard: Things were different when I was in college. Costs were far less. Education was affordable as most people were not going for advanced degrees. Now many jobs that really don't need a masters or a doctorate seem to require one. Plus, private companies during my time at university offered short-term consulting work to PhD candidates so the PhD paid for itself.

Walter: If you were starting your career today, would you have tried to get a PhD?

Richard: Probably not. I don't know why people chase degrees. It wasn't the degree I was trying to get, it was the environment I was trying to find. I think what you're really asking me is why did I choose to work in a university rather than the private sector?

Walter: Yes.

Richard: All I ever wanted to do was work on interesting problems. But it's also fun to work on those problems in an environment where there's time to think. I only found time and quietness in academic math and physics departments. At companies of any size there are so many distractions.

Walter: Sure there are distractions but there's also economic freedom in business. You hear stories all the time of people working a really high paying Wall Street job with the intention to earn a massive amount of money quick and then use the rest of their life to do good with their wealth.

Richard: That's fine if it works out. Remember that the plural of anecdote is not evidence. The two problems with the Wall Street approach are unpredictability and self control.

Walter: What do you mean?

Richard: The outcome of working intensely at a high paying job is much more uncertain that it appears. You might think you can do it for 10 years and then retire a multimillionaire But what if you can't? What if you burn out after wasting all that time without any creative pursuits or personal fulfillment?

Walter: And self control?

Richard: That's the most difficult. Working around money and accumulating a lot very fast requires the self control of frugality. Specifically self control to not increase your quality of living proportionate to your income. This is made harder by the environment. You'll be surrounded by coworkers in pursuit of wealth who earn a lot and spend a lot.

Walter: But if you maintain a simple life, then the upside is enormous. Early wealth can grow and compound for decades.

Richard: Again, I think you're still missing the real question. It isn't "How much money can I earn as fast as possible". It's the question "why work"?

Walter: OK then, why work?

Richard: For me the correct answer is to learn and be creative. When I work I'm creative, which helps me learn, and the more I learn, the more creative I can be, which makes me want to work more.

Walter: Sure, but lots of people are not creative and many people need to work to survive.

Richard: Absolutely right. Which goes back to your first point. You never know why someone works unless you ask them. Everyone has their own reasons and assuming their intentions does them a grave disservice.

I work to be creative. Programming and solving mathematical problems is my art. Luckily they both generate income and serve as a creative pursuit. But when I started out I needed to do jobs that were not as creative, so I balanced work with creativity at home. This is why I wrote books and focused on education in my spare time while doing traditional academic work that paid the bills. Then I gradually merged work and art.

Walter: So is there a time when you'll fully retire and stop working?

Richard: No, I don't think so. I need to work to have a purpose. That's why I still write books. Teaching, writing, and programing are just extensions of myself and my desire to break down every problem to the smallest solvable pieces.

In fact, solving important problems and working on important things helps me solve myself. It's why I suspect so many people define themselves by their work and their career. It's why I can never stop working. Work helps solve the absurdity of the human condition where we have no purpose unless we create one.

While on paternity leave, Walter finished writing a book that introduced computer science principles to young children. Chloe helped illustrate during Cody's nap times and after many revisions, the book was finally ready for self publishing. To get as much feedback as possible, they sent copies to interested friends and family. Walter's work colleagues reviewed all the logic diagrams for clarity. Richard, almost two months late, was the last response the couple needed.

Be on the Bottom of Things

Walter: Richard, I hate to bother you, and I'm sure you're busy, but do you remember getting the email I sent with the pre-print of our children's book?

Richard: Not really. I'm pretty bad with email.

Walter: OK, do you remember the children's book I told you Chloe and I were writing together?

Richard: Of course, the computer science book for kids?

Walter: Yes. We really wanted your feedback and I hadn't heard from you in a few months. Here, I printed out a copy of the book.

Richard: Yes yes! I remember! I really liked the cover, but got so distracted with some other work. Sorry about not responding.

Walter: It's OK. Do you have time to give us feedback? We would really appreciate it. We value your opinion more than anyone on this subject.

Richard: Yes of course I'll read it tonight. Again I apologize for making you wait so long for my response.

One of my good friends and mentors, Don Knuth, always said "My job isn't to be on top of things it's to be on the bottom of them". He used this excuse for why he never read emails.

Richard: I guess you learned well.

Walter: Yes I did, but I feel your pain and I'm sorry for not responding. I'd often be in the same position you're in now. When I needed Don's input, I'd go over to his office and ask for a response. This guy was a legend. He wrote *The Art of Computer Programming* for Christ's sake, so I never really bothered him until absolutely necessary.

I'd remind him about the missed email and he'd let out the loudest laugh. He'd point out that my reminder of what I'd sent by email was proof that he prioritized the correct tasks.

Walter: I suppose if a response was really important, someone will figure out how to get in touch. Which is what I just proved by reminding you.

Richard: Exactly! He also used "getting to the bottom" as a theme for most of his life. He spent his time learning all the first principles of a topic. He'd say "I need to learn the easy stuff the hard way so that I'm prepared for when it gets really hard."

Walter: What does that actually mean?

Richard: It means that he learned every subject that he could from scratch. If he needed to learn a piece of history, he would research the background of everyone involved. If he was learning cryptography he would start with mathematical primitives.

Walter: That seems highly inefficient.

Richard: I agree, he wasted so much time. Which is why I could never get him to respond to an email and he never wanted to be on top of gossip or news or cutting edge research. He only cared about first principles. He only cared about core content and fundamental truths. And his commitment to being out of the loop allowed him to be the only person I knew who truly understood most subjects. He exemplified the difference between knowing the name of something and actually knowing something.

Anyway, that's a side tangent and just an excuse for me being lazy and not reading email. I promise to get you feedback by tomorrow.

Walter: Thanks Richard.

The next morning, Richard returned a marked up version of the children's book to the Carlisles' mailbox. He felt a little uneasy about his edits because of all the red marker that bloodied the pages. At the same time, he and Walter were becoming good friends and he wanted the couple's book to be a success.

Subtract Don't Add

Walter: Thanks so much for the feedback on the manuscript.

Richard: You're welcome. I hope it wasn't too harsh. I'm always a little uneasy providing critiques of others' work. I only feel comfortable editing my own books.

Walter: Harsh? No way! It was very insightful. Unlike most of the other people providing edits you didn't suggest expanding on existing ideas. You mostly just wanted us to delete stuff.

Richard: The content was good but removing extraneous examples helps the really good ideas stand out. Deleting the unnecessary words gives visibility to the really great writing. Especially in a book for young people, you want simplicity.

Walter: Agree. Deleting was a lot easier for us than adding new sections.

Richard: That's great. Most people feel the opposite about deleting because they've created such an emotional attachment to their writing. Deleting feels like throwing out a favorite possession.

Walter: You're right. We did feel as if we wasted time writing the things you wanted us to delete.

Richard: Of course. This is the same feeling you get when you give up a hobby and sell a bass guitar. You're changing your identity, because you had attached yourself to an object or idea.

Walter: Ha! I seem to remember you telling me a story about that before.

Richard: Yes I've learned from experience. Subtraction is always harder but more liberating than addition. Another analogy is going on vacation. People always try and add on a vacation to help relieve stress or make life stressors bearable. Maybe instead of adding on something else they would be happier removing the stress that makes them crave vacation. They would save money, not need the vacation, and improve everyday happiness.

Walter: Wait, you're anti-vacation?

Richard: No, of course not. I'm just a proponent of maximizing daily happiness so a vacation can be something you want to do, not need to do. You must know people who always say, "I really need a vacation". All I'm saying is when you need a vacation you really need to focus on removing stress from daily life.

Walter: Gotcha.

Richard: Anyway, I figured deletion was what you really needed at this point in the process. Nothing is worse than someone telling you to do more work when you're finished. Often what has been done just needs trimming to make perfection.

Walter: Thanks again for reviewing the book.

As Richard became more and more accustomed to life in San Diego, he grew intrigued with local politics. Small scale protests were occurring more frequently. A recent tax hike put increased strain on property owners and businesses. City officials claimed a need to increase taxes to service the large debt incurred during the last financial crisis. In protest, businesses randomly closed for 2-3 days a week to send a message that without them, the city would have nothing. Property taxes were at an all time high delinquency rate. People were angry and locals began to resent the rich moving to the city and building mansions. Almost nightly, there were small-scale protests downtown.

First Principles

Walter: Richard, I've been loving your op-eds in the *Tribune*. How did you get ahold of all those city budgets and project costs?

Richard: Easy, you just go down to city hall and ask. It's an embarrassment that the local media doesn't investigate. Everything is available to the public. It takes a small amount of effort and a few intelligent questions.

Walter: And you knew how to interpret a city financial statement?

Richard: No, but I learned. I just reasoned through it. Economic first principles are very simple.

Walter: First principles?

Richard: Yes, the most basic facts. Break a concept down into the most basic parts and reason from those fundamental truths.

Walter: So why is the city's budget so screwed up?

Richard: Because the mayor and everyone else in charge of the city ignored basic logic. There's a fiscal plan and it's composed of expenses and revenues. For a city, revenue equals taxes. Expenses are everything that the city spends money on. First principles would state that if revenue does not exceed or equal expenses, a city will run a deficit.

But the city also holds assets. Often they borrow money and claim the assets as collateral. The borrowed money helps pay back the old debt but also creates more debt. The more assets, the more a city can borrow.

Walter: And so they got into debt by never having adequate revenue and continuing to borrow?

Richard: Exactly. But this isn't clear to the city's accountants. The more they borrow, the more money they can spend. They build more stuff and pretend to improve the budget because they have more assets to borrow against. But the more they borrow, the more they have to promise to repay with future revenue. And most of the things they build and finance don't bring in additional revenue.

Finances are just addition and subtraction. Nothing more complex than balancing all inputs and all outputs.

Walter: And I'm guessing this is where they defied logic?

Richard: Yes. They define their terms incorrectly so they don't know what to add and what to subtract.

Revenue should balance expenses. If a small deficit is acceptable then occasionally expenses can exceed revenue. The problems occur when accountants define expenses as assets. They make negatives positives.

Walter: You've lost me.

Richard: This city and almost all cities in the U.S. define roads and other infrastructure as assets. This generally accepted accounting principle allows the city to build a road, install water and sewage pipes, construct parks and stadiums, and claim that they increased the value of the assets under management. This makes infrastructure look like a positive when it's really a negative.

The infrastructure costs money to build and continues to cost money to maintain. Infrastructure is a continued expense. But if you treat infrastructure as an asset rather than an expense, then a city can post a stadium as collateral for a loan. A city can essentially be bankrupt but get low interest rate loans by borrowing agains the roads and sewage systems that continue to cost them money. They have to pay the interest on the debt and also pay the maintenance on the so-called assets. Their assets are really liabilities. They have a balance sheet of pure liabilities and nothing but taxes to balance out the massive expenses and debt payments.

They defy basic first principles.

Walter: Isn't this corrupt? I think I heard about this in another state where they had to sell off major highways to a bank that turned it into an expensive toll road.

Richard: It might be corrupt, but as the saying goes, never attribute to malice what can be explained by stupidity.

Walter: So at this point, what can be done to fix the deficit?

Richard: Nothing except bankruptcy. As long as the budget includes more expenses than revenue there is no fix. The biggest problem is that the politicians have no incentive to fix this problem. Their term is finite and they don't need to personally account for the deficits they create. They'll be out of office and long gone before citizens demand accountability.

Just like Upton Sinclair said when running for governor here in California, "It's difficult to get a person to understand something when their salary depends on not understanding."

Walter: Keep writing up your discoveries, everyone I've talked to loves your work.

Richard: Thanks.

Is the effort worth it?

Richard: Hey Walter can I ask you about your startup? I've been reviewing code for the Linux kernel and there was a recent commit from an employee at Giga. Isn't that your company?

Walter: Hardly my company. I just work in the distributive systems division. I think there are close to a thousand employees now.

Richard: OK well this code was written by Naval Patel. Do you know him?

Walter: Yes, very smart guy. He mostly works on firmware and contributes a lot to open source projects. Makes sense that he would be creating pull requests to the linux repository.

Richard: Well, maybe you can put me in touch with him so I can figure out his goals with the proposed code changes. I couldn't find his contact email anywhere. There weren't many comments on his code and I'm having a hard time following his changes. It seems like he created a few incompatibilities with core system calls in order to create a lot of multitasking efficiencies. Do you guys use Linux in all your embedded systems?

Walter: Yes we do. Although it isn't really one of our main focuses these days.

Richard: Oh, you sound disappointed.

Walter: A little bit. The standalone hardware we started making was one of the reasons I joined Giga.

Lately as we get closer and closer to an IPO we've been throwing everything at the wall to see what sticks in order to manufacture as much growth as possible. Please don't tell anyone I've said anything to you, but work is really out of control. Way too much effort for what are minuscule gains in user adoption and growth. I'm pretty exhausted at the end of most days.

Richard: I think this eventually happens at most startups. I dabbled with advising a few young companies and the work seems unnecessarily stressful. I don't understand why it needs to be crazy at work.

Walter: Amen to that. I've tried pitching a slow iterative development cycle but now that we have venture capital funding, the only metric that matters is growth.

Richard: I always told the companies I advised to imagine they were the customer. What would they want? Ideally most people want a product that lasts a long time—is always available if you need to buy again, and has perpetual improvements and support that allows old stuff to continue to work better. New features should only ever improve functionality.

Walter: Yes but once you get venture funding, everything is about user acquisition and lock-in. Keep the customer dependent on your platform and keep getting new users.

Richard: That's the benefit of private self-funded companies. The growth metrics can stay internal and the owners can focus on sustainable values such as customer satisfaction and cash flow. Growth can be slow and natural. Customers stick around because they actually want to, not because they're locked into a platform. And they will be happy to keep buying your products.

Walter: So you agree with me that slow sustainable growth is best? If only I could convince my boss.

Richard: I think a better question is, "What is all that extra effort worth?" At some point more effort and more pressure doesn't create more results. The point of diminishing returns is reached.

Walter: And how do you know if you are at that point?

Richard: Easy, by measuring along the way. The simplest example is with exercise. I love sports involving the water. When I lived in Boulder I was far away from all water sports so I bought a wonderful piece of equipment called a WaterRower. Imagine a rowing machine with a big tank of water that you use for resistance.

Every evening I would get on the rowing machine and row as fast and as hard as I could for 2000 meters. I would do it on my best day in 7 minutes. But after a year or so I started losing motivation to do my 2000 meter daily row.

It wasn't that I stopped enjoying it, but the extreme mental effort of pushing to that time goal eliminated the fun. One day I put on some music and just let my mind wander. When the timer went off at 2000 meters, I looked down at my watch. It was 7 minutes and 15 seconds. All that effort I put into maximizing speed only gave me 15 seconds. From then on I stopped trying to go all out and just went back to having fun.

Walter: So really what you're saying is when performance comes at the expense of fun you've reached a point of diminishing returns.

Richard: Bingo! What does it matter if you achieve all the growth in the world only to burn out and be miserable? Keep a longterm sustainable perspective. Doing your best doesn't necessarily mean getting the maximum result. It can also means doing something for a long time.

Every morning at sunrise, Richard would wake and walk outside with a fresh cup of coffee and inhale the ocean breeze. Then, depending on how his creaky joints felt, he would either put on a wetsuit and walk down to the beach, or sit at a small table, open his laptop and begin writing. Since moving back to the west coast, the salty beach air had invigorated his motivation to write. Over the last few years he had spent most of his educational efforts on podcasting and online videos. Although this translated to the greatest increase in popularity, it often lacked the depth he enjoyed when writing a book or long-form essay.

Chronicle your life

Walter: Hi Richard. Writing as usual?

Richard: Yes sir. I'm about to take a break. This morning was incredibly productive.

Walter: It's good to see you outside writing. I hope it means there'll be a new book out soon that I can read.

Richard: We shall see. It's harder than I thought explaining the power of encryption to the average person. I'm trying my hand at a fictional short story in line with a few of the themes in the book *The Sovereign Individual.* It's very different from what I've written before.

Walter: Interesting, I think I've read a few chapters of *The Sovereign Individual* a long time ago. I remember it during the 2000s when I was in college.

Richard: What are you listening to Walter? You always have your headphones on.

Walter: Just trying to finish an audiobook. It's the biography of Steve Jobs.

Richard: Ah, biographies are funny things. So many people find them inspiring but I'm always left feeling dull. They usually lack emotion and are so predictable.

Walter: What do you mean?

Richard: Many people have biographies and very famous people pay for biographers, but very few write autobiographies. Very few people chronicle their own life, interpret their actions and distill their existence into words and emotional tales. It's a lot of work to write any book, but imagine if you were tasked with writing a book about yourself?

Walter: Well I'm not the right person to ask, my life isn't interesting enough for a biography.

Richard: Exactly wrong! Most people think their life isn't interesting. They think that their life is normal. Almost no one's life is normal and almost everyone has an interesting or useful skill and worldview to share with future generations. Unfortunately none of that information is written and it all dies with the person. Live as if you were tasked with writing an autobiography. At the very least, close friends and family might have an interest in reading your tale.

Walter: Again, I highly doubt anyone would want to read it.

Richard: But what if you had to write one? And you assumed at least one friend and your spouse would read a page or two.

Walter: It would be a very mundane book.

Richard: And this is exactly why you should write an autobiography. It would expose all the areas of life that should be augmented. We live in monotony because we think no one is watching and no one cares. If we knew someone would read our tale we would work as hard as possible to live an exciting life. We would also begin to see excitement in the normal things.

Walter: Isn't this what we see playing out with everyone attempting to photograph and share their life on social media? People want to appear more interesting than they really are.

Richard: To an extent, but posted photos have no context and leave much to the imagination of the viewer. The viewer constructs the narrative of a photo. The writer constructs the narrative of a book.

Walter: I never thought of it that way.

Richard: If you were forced to write an autobiography it would expose all the areas in life considered unimportant. Not only would it empower you to create a narrative around your existence, it would help you thread meaning through the events you consider normal. You would start to question your decisions if others would later read about your choices.

Walter: This reminds me a little of journaling.

Richard: Journals are overrated. No one ever reads a journal. Instead of spending time writing something no one will read, write an autobiography with the intent of distributing your book to the people you care about.

Walter: So, have you written your autobiography?

Richard: Of course. I'm always adding to it. When I die, my tale of struggles and successes will be released to the public automatically on my website.

Limited Resources

Richard: Walter, you inspired me to read a little about Steve Jobs. I was surprised to find out how highly he valued time. I'm always fascinated with people who understand the importance of time.

He seemed to value time over money. One of the articles I read was in *Playboy* where he basically said that his favorite things don't cost any money, they just require time. I never realized he was so aware of money's limitations.

Walter: I guess you're one of the few who actually read *Playboy* for the articles.

Richard: Don't make me blush.

Walter: His biography also mentioned how he seemed to care more about experiences and creativity than money. I guess he used money to free up time so he could do what he wanted.

Richard: I suppose so. Time is one of the few provably scarce resources. It's truly non-renewable.

Walter: Yeah, recently I heard a remarkable fact. If you live 75 years you barely have 650,000 hours of life. And, you spend a third of that sleeping. And another ten to fifteen percent working. That leaves very little left over for everything else.

Richard: And when we work, we exchange our very limited time on earth for money.

Walter: It's a wonder anyone works.

Richard: Well, work is more than just a means of acquiring money, but yes, many people quit dead-end jobs because they come to this realization. We should all guard our time. Wasting time is one of life's greatest crimes.

Walter: I struggle with this idea a lot ever since we had Cody and especially now that Chloe is pregnant again.

Richard: Wow, that's great! I haven't seen Chloe recently, so I didn't even realize you guys were expecting.

Walter: Thank you. Children really bring awareness to a parent's mortality. Especially during a chaotic work week when I see my coworkers more than my family, I really question where I'm spending my time. Programming for a large company is exceptionally hard because so much of my time gets wasted. We work on a project for a few months only to have specs change or get new growth metrics that cause the team to focus on a new strategic direction. We scrap a lot of code and start fresh, erasing hours of work.

Richard: Well, you need to give purpose to those hours and if you can't find purpose perhaps it isn't a great job even if the pay is good. The problem spans both ways. People trade rare hours for low paying jobs, or waste their hours on frivolous purchases just as often as people waste their life in dull uninspiring high paying jobs. Very few people realize the time value of money. If they did they certainly wouldn't want to receive dollars for their labor.

Walter: What do you mean? If you're not paid in dollars what would you be paid with?

Richard: Gold would be fine. Something that cannot easily be inflated. Sometime stock is ok as well. If I give limited time for an unlimited dollar that can be printed at will then I'm really selling myself short. But if I give my time for a limited resource then I'm at least receiving fair value for my precious time on earth.

Walter: Speaking of all this, did you you see the stock market today?

Richard: No what happened? I don't really follow the market on a daily basis.

Walter: There was a huge crash. Apparently some of the major banks might be insolvent. The government is providing a multi-trillion dollar bailout.

Richard: This is my point exactly! You shouldn't be surprised. Dollars can be created out of thin air.

Walter: I'm not surprised, but you're right. Every once in a while the government seems to conjure money to bail out too big to fail companies.

Richard: Yes, it's a silly proposition to give away your time for dollar bills that can be created by the federal reserve with a few key strokes. That's why everyone accumulates wealth in real-estate and holds stocks and bonds in their retirement accounts.

Walter: Oh don't bring up my retirement, I just lost a bunch in my 401k after this crash.

Richard: Don't worry about it. You aren't retiring anytime soon.

Walter: Sure but on paper it still hurts a little to look at the balance.

Richard: Have you ever thought about what money really is?

Walter: As in what is a dollar bill? I guess at the end of the day it's just a piece of paper we believe in.

Richard: Not really. I've found that almost no one really understands money. Some of the smartest minds in the world have no idea what it means to be paid for work. I actually don't even using the term, "earning money," instead I call it "trading for money".

When a company wants me to consult on a big engineering project, I think about how much time I would be willing to trade for the money they offer. If the project is incredibly exciting I'm less interested in the money because I'm also trading time for fun.

Walter: Sure, but you're just talking about valuing your time. That doesn't really explain money. Besides, money is a method of them transferring value to you for what you've done.

Richard: No, money is more than a means of sending value from one person to another. Money is a ruler. It's a standard for measuring the value of time.

The most limited resource on the planet is an individuals' time. Time is non-renewable and should be valued at the highest price. If I live to be 85 years old, I'll only be alive for 31,025 days. If I trade my time for dollars and those dollars decreases in value I've been robbed of some of my precious hours of life.

Walter: Of course, that's inflation. And that's why you never keep too much cash sitting around, it's always losing value.

Richard: It's inflation that makes our current money so dishonest. It robs people of time. It steals from those who trade time for dollars.

This is the disturbing part of most of the world's economies. In developing countries, a new government steps in and changes the money or inflates it away, destroying life savings. In the US, a new spending bill dumps billions or trillions into the economy all under the guise of stimulus. Most people don't realize that everyday they trade time for money. They are trading their life for money. If money is devalued, then they are robbed of a small piece of their life.

Walter: Right, but stimulus can help keep countries out of depressions. Sometimes we need the government's help.

Richard: Of course the economy needs an intervention every once in a while, but debasing the money steals from those who hold the currency. Extra money in the economy leads to an increase in assets like stocks, bonds, houses and other rare things that serve longterm savings. The inflation creates a dollar that is neither a good store of value or a long term medium of exchange.

Walter: So what would you do? How could you prevent inflation?

Richard: If you had no new money creation then your dollar would continuously purchase more and more the longer you chose to not spend it.

Walter: And that would be deflation?

Richard: Yes.

Walter: And ultimately deflation is better than inflation?

Richard: I think most normal people would want to buy more with their dollar over time rather than less.

Walter: But presumably you would get paid less over time as well if the dollar kept increasing in value.

Richard: Sure, but as manufacturing efficiency increased, more goods would be produced at less expense. Just think of the price on TVs. They're not less expensive because the dollar is more valuable, they're less expensive because we make them more efficiently with better manufacturing. This principle applies to all technology products. Every year if you wait, you will get more for your money. Phones and laptops are always getting faster and faster but the price either stays the same or decreases. Good and services should always decrease in price because we get more and more efficient.

Walter: And this is why you like gold? Because it protects against inflation?

Richard: Of course. I always tried to negotiate to get paid in ounces of gold.

Walter: Ha! No way! You got PBS to pay you in gold when you did your TV series?

Richard: Even better! I got them to pay me in bitcoin. There will never be more than 21 million bitcoin so at least I traded my limited time for something equally as limited.

Richard and Chloe had their daughter Mia just as their son Cody turned 3. Fortunately, the Carlisles finished their small home office addition just in time. Next door, Richard also finally furnished his house, giving it a spartan beach bum vibe. He even extended his front porch so he could cook outside on a gas range. Now, in addition to drinking coffee outside every morning, he also cooked breakfast. As he grew more comfortable on his little plot of land, he immersed himself in gardening with the creation of a fully automated sprinkler system using local weather forecasts and environmental sensors. His front lawn quickly became a lush tropical oasis.

Finding Time

Walter: Hey Richard, do you have a minute?

Richard: Of course.

Walter: Oh wow, the pepper and banana plants are really looking good. I love how the neighborhood smells like a breakfast diner every morning you cook out here. Strong work.

Richard: Thanks, this is certainly the most expensive pepper I'll ever eat, considering the amount of effort it took to create a garden. But home automation has come a long way and this irrigation system was a lot of fun to tinker with. What's on your mind?

Walter: I've been working on a few side projects at home, and I'm increasingly frustrated with not being able to finish them. I just wanted to ask your advice. When you had a young family and were working on your research, how did you ever make time to write your first book?

Richard: I didn't make any time, I just found wasted time.

I never really watched much television but in the evenings when everyone was asleep I'd often watch a movie. So, I just stopped watching movies and reclaimed about 1-2 hours a day. I still needed more time so instead of waking up at 7 AM, drinking coffee and reading the news, I woke up at 6 AM and drank coffee while writing. But, it still wasn't enough.

After waking at 6 AM every day for a few months, I pushed a little harder and tried to wake up at 5 AM. But I couldn't do it. My body really hated super early mornings. So, I compromised with my biology and worked on the book every weekday starting at 5:30 AM.

I also found a big chunk of time I was saving for relaxation on weekend mornings. I loved staying up late and sleeping in, but at the end of the day I found I couldn't write at night. Only the morning hours suited my mind's focus. So, begrudgingly but determined I woke everyday as early as possible while the house was quiet. In the evenings, I would often reread what I wrote in the morning. Slowly over the course of a year, I recovered a lot of hours.

Walter: That's a really impressive push to get your book done. I tend to be the opposite. I'd rather work late at night.

Richard: The biggest thing to realize is how much time is strewn around your life like spare change. We frequently discard time as if we had unlimited quantities. Finding it is only a third of the battle. The other two parts involve reclaiming it and then stopping yourself from continually discarding it. Whenever I see someone with true mastery, I don't ever say, "Wow, they must be really exceptional". Instead I say, "Wow, they must be really good at not wasting time".

Do you think incredible athletes waste time reading the news? No way. Not only do they use brain cycles to constantly think about their goal, they reclaim scattered time so they can prioritize their work. Most elite professionals do nothing more than one or two things over and over again all day everyday.

Walter: That might be easier said that done. I'm already up in the morning helping with the newborn and already exhausted at the end of the day cleaning up the house and finishing small amounts of programming and debugging that I bring home from the office.

Richard: I bet there is some time you can reclaim. And if there isn't, maybe the new project isn't the best use of your time. Or maybe the some of the requirements for your time need to be paused.

Always remember, whenever you aren't being productive, someone else is.

Doing the Uncomfortable

Richard: Good morning Walter! You guys should come over. I just made some incredible pancakes.

Walter: You want pancakes, Cody?

Cody: YES!

Richard: Awesome. Cody, where's your Mom and sister? They're invited for breakfast too.

Cody: Mommy's taking care of Mia. She's fussy.

Walter: Yeah Mia was up all night so they are both sleeping now.

Richard: Glad they're getting some peace and quiet then.

Walter: I think we should eat outside. We can be pretty messy.

Richard: Of course, I'm keeping them warm on the outdoor stove. One of the best purchases I've made in a long time.

Walter: I'm very impressed. You're more domesticated than you initially let on.

Richard: Thanks. I'm not as absent minded as I look. Hey, after we talked yesterday I thought about the time I spent writing my first book a little more.

When I started out writing, I frequently stopped to attend to distractions, especially if I encountered a challenging topic.

In my first book, *The Everything Theory*, I could never get past the chapter on chaos in biology without washing dishes, cleaning the table, fixing a burned out lightbulb, or doing countless other productive procrastination activities around the house. I realized it was mentally uncomfortable for me to tackle the hard problem of writing that section, so I simply distracted myself with other seemingly important tasks.

If my goal was to write a book, then these small chores were not productive, they were wasting reclaimed time. I wasn't waking up at 5:30 in the morning to wash dishes or change a lightbulb, I was waking up to finish my book! My solution was a little trick that I later tried to teach all of my students. I call it “doing the uncomfortable”.

Walter: So how does it work?

Richard: When faced with a challenge while working, you'll be tempted to busy yourself with something easy. When writing, you won't know what to say or how to rephrase a sentence and you'll open a new web-browser tab or check your phone.

Instead, focus on the uncomfortable feeling and don't do anything else. Force yourself to embrace the difficult task, at least for a few minutes longer than normal. The mind is plastic and can be adapted to almost any situation. If you focus only on the challenge and avoid temptation for easy distraction, you can strengthen your resolve. Eventually this uncomfortable feeling becomes the feeling you enjoy and you gain an ability to focus that few people ever master.

I later learned that many athletes use this technique when training. At the physical limit, they push for one more repetition. It's like doing one more pushup or pull-up right at the point of breaking, or programing for just 5 minutes longer before getting a new cup of coffee. Doing one more of whatever you're doing puts you in a position to build mental strength in challenging situations.

The longer you're uncomfortable, the less uncomfortable the thing becomes. Then it takes more and more to make you uncomfortable and you start performing at higher and higher levels.

Walter: That's interesting. I'll have to give it a try. Lately, I work with my wifi turned off so that I can't distract myself with news or email.

Cody: Daddy Daddy Daddy!

Walter: What Cody? What?

Cody: I'm done! Are we ready to go to the store?

Walter: Yes, I think so. Thanks, Richard, for second breakfast. We're going on a walk to pick up some groceries. Do you need anything?

Richard: No I'm OK, thanks. Enjoy the morning.

In the evening, with the children in bed, Walter would occasionally lay out in the front yard on the hammock strung between two palms. On a clear starlight evening, he'd drink a local beer and look up at the sky wondering if some of the extra bright dots were satellites. Many times he'd catch Richard outside as well, reclining in an Adirondack chair, face illuminated by the screen of his e-reader.

Plans

Richard: Nice night?

Walter: Yes. It's times like these when I never want to live anywhere else.

Richard: Couldn't agree more. Cool salty air and clear skies. By the way, shouldn't you be taking advantage of quiet time at home and finishing one of those nagging projects?

Walter: Maybe one day I'll get to your level of discipline and skill at reclaiming time. Just like you said, if there is no time, or not enough motivation, a side project might just need to wait. Until Chloe finishes her master's, I'm just spread too thin with both our kids and work. On a night like tonight I'd much rather just chill.

Richard: Nothing helps you learn the importance of relaxing your plans more than children. I'm type A to the extreme. When Janice and I had children, I couldn't adjust to the chaos. I relied on a very structured schedule when doing research. I applied the strict scheduling of my work to planning events for my kids. But children don't abide by strict schedules. They have no filter and are not afraid to tell you what is and isn't fun.

I clearly remember one day when Janice was working an extra shift at the hospital and I was on solo parent duty. I planned two activities, the children's museum if it rained, or the zoo if sunny. The next morning was beautifully sunny so we all piled into the car with snacks, and headed to the zoo. When we arrived, we parked on the edge of a large park that we'd cut through to save time. A minute into our walk both James and Zoe wanted to swing. Checking my watch I pushed them on the swings and tried to encourage only a short diversion from my master zoo plan.

Thinking about the time and our need to get to the zoo, I kept missing Zoe's imaginary story about the neighborhood trash truck. This frustrated her and she kept yelling, "Dad, pay attention." Then as we left the swings, James started chasing a squirrel while Zoe followed with a large stick exclaiming she was the queen of the world.

Realizing that my plans were foiled for a zoo excursion I gave in to their imagination. We spent a whole hour trying to skip rocks at a small pond. Then we found a shady spot to eat the food I packed. We even made dandelion crowns as we wandered back to our car. Both kids were exhausted and I had to carry them upstairs for their afternoon nap. When they woke they talked about our morning adventure for the rest of the day. Weeks later they kept bringing up in conversation the wonderful "travel through the magic-land" we experienced that day.

Plans are excellent but don't let them suppress possibility. I could never have planned such a wonderful day for my kids. And if I had firmly stuck to my plan, I would have ruined their day.

Walter: That makes me feel better for relaxing when I should be doing something.

Richard: Don't ever feel bad enjoying life.

Walter: Right now there are things more important than my small home-brew software idea. And when there are less important things to do, my project will be most important, and I'll finally get around to it.

Richard: Always reprioritize your life. Have a loose framework, flexible plans, and follow the fun.

Work Goals

Walter: Hey Richard, remember last weekend you told me the story of your kids and the zoo outing?

Richard: Of course.

Walter: Well it really resonated with me. It got me thinking about work and life in general.

Richard: How so?

Walter: Well I originally had the goal of getting a position at a fast growing tech startup, enduring the stress, working day in day out, sleeping under my desk, watching the company IPO and cashing out with huge gains. Then I'd use my earnings to start my own company.

Richard: What changed?

Walter: To be honest, I had two kids. I've also lost interest working at Giga ever since the executives began considering the IPO timeframe. I really dislike spending so many weekends away from home and missing out on family events. I think I've been trying to find time for side projects because of my unhappiness at work.

Richard: It's really good to hear you have such insight. My children, without knowing, taught me one of the most valuable lessons of my career: spontaneity. I stopped being rigid in my goals of advancement within the mathematics department at Berkeley and my work at Livermore. I lost interest in playing the game of academia with promotion, tenure, committee appointments, and all of the other annoying aspects of professorship.

I started working on more and more projects outside of the university. Teaching my children made me realize I loved explaining science to others more than I enjoyed publishing ideas in a journal. I started teaching at a local high school summer camp. I began working on my second book, *The Chaotic Life,* so I could explain chaos theory and complex systems to the masses. Really, I just started having fun again. My original goals were getting in the way of enjoyment. But without my kids, I never would have realized I needed to quit my job.

So maybe some of the time spent with your children will paradoxically help you find time for other projects.

Walter: Interesting way to think about it. I'm not sure I can just quit. Maybe if I didn't have kids and didn't need the steady income, I could dabble more with side projects and freelance work. But not at this stage of life.

Richard: So many of my colleagues were childless. I realized that without the craziness of parenting it's very easy to get wrapped up in your own self-importance. The plans that you originally laid out become rigid and permanent because nothing ever forces change.

Kids, on the other hand, have this way of breaking your habits, breaking your expectations, and more importantly breaking your sense of self.

Walter: I still don't fully get what you're saying. How did your kids make you feel free enough to leave your job? I feel the opposite. I'm more fearful of change since I need the stability of employment to support my family.

Richard: My kids didn't make me feel as if I could quit, they made me realize I needed to quit. My children made me reevaluate my priorities and interests. Writing stale research publications was nowhere near as fun as teaching my children about gravity and relativity. Watching their excitement when they solved a logic puzzle I created, gave me happiness in excess of any publication in *Nature*.

Just like you, I was very concerned about steady and predictable income but my work goals had changed and I developed an adversity to wasting time in meetings. I bet you have as well, especially if it makes you late coming home to your family.

Walter: Yes.

Richard: So in my case, I was keenly aware that I needed income for my family. I also knew because of my children, that I couldn't afford to waste any time. I wanted to spend as much of it as I could with them, while continuing to work on interesting problems.

My kids made me realize how much I loved teaching science. While employed at a university, as you know, I wrote my first book. It did modestly well. I hedged my bets and waited until I had a way of stepping out of my academic job and pursing a new career aligned with my new goals.

Once I had some income from writing I felt free to venture out as a consultant. This gave me greater flexibility with work hours and more family time. Consulting also provided me variety. I could work on computer science and physics projects without a university labeling me as unfocused. By chance, consulting also earned more money than pursing a stodgy tenured professorship.

Walter: So your advice is quit only when you have a decent second option?

Richard: That's always a good idea. But a better way to sum up what I'm saying is, constantly evaluate your life. Sometimes the correct option is to quit, other times keep going. When your actions show that your goals have changed, don't naively stick with old goals that no longer fit with your life's needs. There is no shame in quitting and there is no failure in changing your mind. Goals are not forever and goals should never feel binding.

One morning after ignoring the weather advisories and feeling eager to surf a massive swell, Richard returned from the beach with a torn wetsuit and broken board. Leaving the board on the front lawn in pieces, he showered and scrubbed his bloodied knee. After reemerging with a fresh set of shorts he sat on his front step and bandaged his cuts and scrapes. Looking up at the stormy sky, he was thankful he hadn't died in the incredibly violent ocean. He had been careless and overconfident and the forces of nature humbled him.

Skipping Out

Walter: Richard, you look bad. What happened to your board?

Richard: Hey Walter. I cracked it this morning. The surf was far too rough and I should have listened to you when you warned me yesterday.

Walter: Your knee looks pretty banged up too.

Richard: Yeah I took quite a tumble near some rocks. It really shook me up.

Walter: Heal up fast. Take a break, you aren't as young as you think you are. I'll see you in a few days. I'm waiting for a ride to pick me up for the airport.

Richard: Where are you going?

Walter: There's a large data mining conference in San Francisco so I'll be there for the next two days. Work is paying me to train on two new statistical packages for R. Chloe's sister is staying with us to help with the kids.

Richard: Have fun. One of my favorite life hacks is skipping out of conferences that I agreed to attend.

Walter: Of course you'd say that.

Richard: I used to attend 3-4 conferences per year. Originally for my university job then just to network and grow my consulting opportunities. Rarely was I presenting on a subject and I just used the conferences as a common meeting place for regrouping with distant colleagues. After a few years I grew increasingly bored with conferences due to the monotony and the fact that all of the information gets shared online.

Walter: Yes, but sometimes they're a nice excuse to get a break from family chaos.

Richard: Of course. I kept going to conferences long after I grew bored with them. But as soon as I arrived, I'd skip out on everything except a few social activities. I used my time away from home to work on projects in my hotel room.

These were some of the most productive times, because I reserved time, had minimal distractions and intense focus. Occasionally I'd try and trick myself by planning a trip to a different city with no conference and stay in my hotel room and work. I'm not sure why, but it was never as productive as skipping out on the real conferences.

Walter: Tricking the mind is a difficult thing. This conference won't be one I can skip since there's a training session each morning I need to attend. But for the rest of the presentations, I'll probably take your advice.

Richard: Is this your car pulling up?

Walter: Looks like it.

Richard: Enjoy the trip, I'll be shopping for a new longboard and maybe a cane while you're gone.

It was late when Walter returned from his two day conference San Francisco. As he walked from the corner where the driver dropped him off, he stopped at Richard's gate. The faint sound of heavy metal guitar came from Richard's open front window as Walter decided to bring the package left on the sidewalk up to the porch. He needed an excuse to ask Richard's opinion of a new brain-computer interface startup that offered him a job. Through the screen door, he saw Richard sitting on the floor staring at a projection that filled his entire kitchen wall. As Walter knocked, Richard waved him in without turning away from his work.

Making a change

Walter: I didn't take you for a heavy metal fan?

Richard: Well, some problems need a certain mood.

Walter: What am I looking at on your wall?

Richard: This is a spec for a new open hardware single board computer. It's actually the same one I used in my garden irrigation system. Now that the U.S. has a non-profit-funded semiconductor foundry it's possible to create hardware on home soil. No more need to outsource the silicon production. The designer wanted me to help him with some heat issues. Occasionally it will reset during a hot day. If we can get it right, this will be incredible for hobbyists and builders. One hundred times the performance of a Raspberry Pi but probably only a few dollars more in cost.

Walter: And you helped create this?

Richard: No. A researcher in Reno did all the designing. What brings your over? I'm judging by your suitcase that you didn't come over just to chat about this little experimental computer.

Walter: No, you're right. I was bringing up this package left outside your gate. I also needed your opinion. I was offered a job by a really interesting startup working on human brain interfaces. The only issue is that I would have to move to Dallas. Have you heard of anything promising with implantable computers?

Richard: Sorry, not particularly. But moving is a big deal. What does Chloe think?

Walter: She isn't thrilled. I briefly told her about it on the phone and haven't really had a chance to talk through the details. Texas is a little too humid for her.

Richard: Have you spent a lot of time with the people and looked through their tech?

Walter: A small amount. They had some demos at the conference. I didn't want to put too much time into investigating if Chloe wasn't first on board with the idea of moving.

Richard: I evaluate a change on a small scale first before fulling committing. Take a family trip to Dallas. If you can't handle a week in Dallas then it's unlikely you'll want to live there all year round.

Walter: Good point. Maybe I'll propose a short vacation.

Richard: When Janice and I decided to move with our children to Boulder after I decided to leave academia we didn't just move across the country and buy a new house. We decided to take a few two-week vacations. Staying in a rental house with our children and pretending that we lived in a new city let us all feel comfortable when we finally moved.

I've done the same thing with most life changes, big or small.

Walter: Basically you're telling me to take baby steps.

Richard: Absolutely. Never make a change all at once. If the change is a terrible idea with a small commitment, you'll only lose a small amount of time or effort.

I never really know if a choice is good until I try it on a small scale. Just like running an experiment, you don't apply for a million-dollar grant to test a hypothesis, you run a small pilot trial and see if there is any signal worth pursuing. You don't just put your whole net worth into a good stock one day, you dollar cost average.

This has also made it easy for me to try new things very frequently by continuously making small changes. I can make a lot of small quick changes to my life and if they work out on a short term basis then I will stick with them for the long term effects.

Walter: And I guess you can also fail fast and painlessly.

Richard: Exactly right.

Heeding Richard's advice, Walter took a trip to Dallas, first by himself to see the new startup and then with the family to explore the city. Nothing felt right about the job or the location. Still feeling the need to make a change, he responded to a local recruiter's posting for a new cloud computing job at Tenex, and was offered a position. The new position, although exciting, paid substantially less but offered additional compensation through stock options. The financial tightening coupled with two young children caused significant home stress.

On Meditation

Richard: Why so glum?

Walter: I guess my poker face isn't as good as I thought. Home life has been complete chaos.

Richard: Are the kids doing OK?

Walter: Yes, the kids are fine. But ever since the city's finances imploded, a lot of the daycares receiving public funding have temporarily closed. Turns out, our daycare and pre-K were subsidized by the city's education fund. Now the kids are home all the time and everything is crazy. I mostly work from home while the remodeling finishes at our headquarters so I need to balance the kids and work. Telecommuting is nice in theory, but in practice it's impossible with everyone running around the house.

Richard: You and Chloe hanging in there?

Walter: We're on each other's nerves, but I guess we're surviving. I made the situation worse by taking the job at Tenex and essentially cutting my monthly pay. Financial tightening, one salary, and no childcare is a recipe for stress.

Richard: But Tenex is giving you get great stock options right?

Walter: Yes but Chloe really insists on an emergency fund and she isn't pleased that we're now living paycheck to paycheck. Much of my earnings are tied up in these long term options. It sounded good on paper but maybe was a bad idea in hindsight. When you take away one person's income, the mortgage and student loan burden really becomes evident.

Richard: There's a real problem with the level of debt piled on top of young people these days.

Walter: Yes, I can't wait to have my student loans paid off.

Richard: So Chloe's not getting paid during the school closure?

Walter: She's furloughed right now since the city budget called for partial school closures. Her middle school was one of the locations selected in the lottery to close. As a compromise with the teacher union's demands for pension guarantees they made the class sizes bigger and gave some teachers extra unemployment pay. Until her school opens back up she's at home. If the budget gets fixed and everything opens after Christmas she'll go back to work. Fortunately, this made her available to take care of the kids while I work, but it means she bears the brunt of all the home stressors. It's created some resentment towards me getting to work all day while she struggles with an infant and a 3 year old.

Richard: Wow, I didn't know it was that crazy. Working from home is nice, but not with a house full of kids. I guess you can't really get them out of the house since all public parks and libraries are closed too, right?

Walter: Pretty much the whole city is hollowed out with every public employee temporarily unemployed. Apparently even the buses stopped running so people aren't showing up for work at some places. Chloe's handling it much better than me. She has a calmness about the whole situation and keeps claiming her morning meditation helps keep everything in perspective as the day gets crazy.

Richard: Have you tried meditation?

Walter: A few times, but I don't see how sitting in my closet quietly helps me stay calm as the day gets difficult. Is meditation something you do?

Richard: Not any more. Don't get me wrong, I did try in the past and even attended a silent retreat. The retreat was enjoyable, but mainly as a time to think without interruption. Contrary to the popular view that meditation helps cultivate mindfulness, I never found the practice helped me much on a daily basis. Seemed like a better use of my time to be in challenging situations and try and control my emotions under stress.

When meditating, I always felt like a football player training all day in the gym but never playing in the game. I found it better to be out on the field and practice emotional control where it mattered rather than sitting still in a quiet place aware of my chaotic mind.

Walter: Don't get me in trouble, but I told Chloe the same thing. I can meditate all I want but when a stressful event occurs practicing in a peaceful spot doesn't seem to help me keep my cool. The mindfulness meditation in my closet provides little to no help. Practicing calmness and awareness during the day is a different story.

Richard: I actually wrote about this exact issue with meditation a few years ago on my blog. Everyone was into meditation apps and courses at the time and I felt the need to reset the public's expectations of meditation. Contrary to what some meditation proponents want you to believe, meditation does not fix everything.

Walter: Does it fix anything?

Richard: Meditation's value comes from its difficulty. It's hard to sit still and be aware of your intrinsically chaotic mind. Most people don't realize they have an out of control mind, so meditation lets them pull back the curtain on their racing and often random thoughts. For the first time, when meditating, they see the craziness of the monkey mind and if they're attentive, will realize how little control they have over their brains' activity.

Walter: Of course.

Richard: Meditation doesn't make you a better person. I don't think meditation actually solves any problem. If you are a terrible person before meditating and you create a daily practice around meditation, you'll still be a terrible person that just happens to be good at meditation.

Walter: So what's the point of meditation?

Richard: The point is to stop trying to control everything. Meditation reveals how little control we have over our brain's activity. We are just responding to a cacophony of random thoughts. When you meditate you get the opportunity to be aware of what is happening inside your skull while forcing yourself to sit. The only thing meditation teaches is patience in the face of a lack of control. It is one of the best ways to observe the mess that is the human brain. But once you realize there are a lot of things outside of your control it is best to practice calmness in the real world.

In the Present

Walter: I read your blog post on meditation.

Richard: That's great, did it help at all?

Walter: It did, but not in the way I expected.

Richard: What do you mean?

Walter: I expected you to explain why meditation doesn't fix everything and can't serve as a magic bullet, but instead you mostly wrote about the power of being aware of the present.

Richard: Yes, present awareness is the single most important thing I've ever learned. Nothing has helped me feel more peacefull. Once I realized that the future and the past don't exist, everything started to make sense. Only the present exists. Looking back, I realized I wrote the piece on meditation with the tone of a self help guru, but I couldn't find a better way to explain my thoughts.

Walter: I'm still a little confused on that point. I understand being aware of the present, but don't really understand your reasoning with the past and future not existing.

Richard: The possibilities of the future exist. But at this moment, the only reality is the present. All future events are possibilities. All past events are memories.

Walter: And how does awareness of past and present not existing help you?

Richard: The present is not only the most important moment it is the only moment we have to act. It means that if I behave poorly, I'm wasting the only time I have. It means I have no choice but to behave well because if I don't I could bring a worse future into existence.

I approach it mathematically. The future is just a series of possibilities not yet actualized. And those possibilities are dependent on what I do now. If I do something dumb like yell and scream, then I increase the chances that future events will be more stressful. If I respond calmly I might bring a calm future into existence.

Walter: That sounds all well and good as a theory but I don't see how knowing the present is all that exists will help me stay calm in a time of stress.

Richard: You're right. It isn't just about knowing, it's about acting on what you know. If all you have is the present moment, then losing your cool in a time of stress is a colossal waste.

Of course it's inevitable that you'll fail to stay calm and make a mess every once in a while, but if you view these actions as failures then you'll be less likely to do it again. If optimizing the present moment is really important, messing up should lead to a feeling of disappointment. After being disappointed with yourself multiple times, a change in your behavior should eventually occur.

Walter: And what happens if my disappointment doesn't lead to a change in action. Do you think meditation could help improve my chances of success?

Richard: I doubt it. You don't need to meditate to be aware of the importance of the present. I think this is why meditation can be a hindrance for many people. They meditate but then never actualize their practice. For many, meditation is procrastination under the guise of self improvement. They focus on being good at meditation but not being better at life.

Goals that don't cause action are a huge problem. Only the plans that cause immediate action are worthwhile. All other goals are just imaginary thoughts. If you have a goal of remaining calm and considerate during difficult times but never really work towards improving your actions, is it really a goal? Or are you just lying to yourself?

Walter: Again, I don't see how this helps me be less stressed and aggravated.

Richard: Well, is being less emotionally volatile a good goal?

Walter: Yes of course it is.

Richard: So if you have the goal to be less emotional during a time of stress you have to commit to acting on that goal. This means practicing calmness under stress, receiving feedback and recording successes. Approach it like any new skill. Constant spaced repetition with measurement and focus. If you can't continue to improve your emotional control, you have to be honest with yourself about the importance of the goal.

Think about going to the bathroom. Do you debate about going? Do you read about it and spend time thinking about all of the times you need to use the bathroom throughout the day? No. You just go right away because you don't want to pee your pants. But in the beginning of your life, you practiced going to the bathroom a lot and eventually you didn't need to wear a diaper.

Walter: So after being aware of my shortcomings over and over again I will finally fix them?

Richard: No you're still missing the point. You act on it now. Don't just be aware of your shortcomings, practice improving them until they become a habit.

Walter: So in this case I need to be constantly aware of my tendency to get mad at the kids disrupting my work so that when they inevitably barge into my office during a conference call I respond appropriately.

Richard: Yes, this is self awareness. No amount of meditation will help you act better. You simply have to act better by trying to act better. You take feedback from the times you fail and incorporate that into your response. Regardless of whether you decide mediation is useful, you need to constantly tweak your actions. This helps you improve.

Eventually your response becomes habituated and correct. Just like using the bathroom. Then you move on to improving another area of your life. Some people find sitting quietly and being aware of their thoughts a way of channeling this energy. I found being aware of the immediacy of the present and desire for a good future the only way to improve my actions and thoughts.

Walter: So walk me through this? I am in a stressful event and I am supposed to reflexively think of being calm.

Richard: No you need to practice being calm by intentionally putting yourself in stressful situations. You go into the game with the intent of winning. And when you lose you do a play-by-play analysis to identify areas for improvement. This means immerse yourself in childcare rather than fleeing from it. If the kids cause you anxiety, spend more time with them. Initially you will pretend to be calm, then after pretending to be calm enough times, you'll actually be calm. Just like any important problem, you solve it by daily immersion.

As you constantly practice emotional calmness in difficult situations, self control becomes easier and easier. Even now, you're conditioning your brain for calmness because you're thinking about it. This makes staying calm much easier the next time something unnerving occurs. At the beginning, however, you need to fake it until you make it.

Walter: What a counseling session! Thanks Richard.

Richard: You're welcome. I only learned this by being in your shoes for the first ten years of my marriage. I spent a lot of time at the office so I could avoid home stress until I realized avoidance didn't help me get better. I was wasting the present by not immersing myself in the stressful events I was avoiding. I embraced the uncomfortable feeling and was better because of it.

Walter: Thanks again.

Richard: Anytime. And congrats on the new job.

After eight months of frozen city spending, a state bailout package paired with clever accounting allowed for a resumption of all public services. Bad scheduling, however, left Chloe working parent teacher conferences at the same time Walter had to stay late at work. Coupled with a last minute cancelation from their babysitter, the Carlisles had to ask Richard if he could watch the kids. When the kids heard that Richard was coming over, they were thrilled. They loved him. His spontaneous deliveries of ice-cream and cookies to the Carlisle's house had made him quiet popular among the kids, not to mention the frequent porch breakfasts and sand toys he brought down for beach picnics.

Imagining like a child

Richard: Welcome back guys. Sorry to whisper but I never got Cody and Mia up to bed. They're both asleep in the living room.

Walter: Oh no problem. Chloe is coming up behind me. She is just putting some things away in the garage and will help carry everyone upstairs. Did the kids do OK?

Richard: Yeah we played some board games and did a lot of hide and seek.

Walter: I still can't believe I had a world renowned mathematician watch my children while I was at work. I really appreciate you filling in. Our newest babysitter is really unreliable. We're going to have to replace her.

Richard: It wasn't a problem at all. I had a wonderful time. It has been awhile since I've had the chance to simply take care of kids. Pure imaginary relaxation.

Walter: Relaxation? I've never heard that word describe my kids.

Richard: Relaxation in the sense that there is no need to be uptight or self conscious. A child doesn't care if you fart when running behind a couch or if you have a mustard stain on your shorts.

The more I played with my children, the more and more I practiced imagining the world like a child. Some people simply think children daydream but a child's mind doesn't have any preconceived notion of true or false. Everything is simultaneously true and false at the same time.

Walter: Well if you like playing with my kids so much you should watch them more often.

Richard: Of course, I'd be glad to. It made me remember when I used to walk around with my son and daughter in the park and they would ask questions like, "Why is the tree brown and not yellow". "Why are my feet on my legs and not my head"? My kids would laugh and laugh and I would actually try and imagine an alternative world in which many things were different. If you don't find a babysitter, I'd be thrilled to help out anytime. Tonight was wonderful in a very simple way.

Walter: Well of course, I just always assumed you were too busy.

Richard: I'm never too busy for children. Playing with kids helps fill a few personal holes. I never imagined that one day I would live alone without my wife and kids. Perhaps playing silly imagination games when they were really young prepared me subconsciously. Maybe it helped me imagine the world differently and know that I could adapt to anything regardless of how hard.

On a more positive note, remind me some time to tell you about the craziness of serving on the Colorado state commission for science textbook selection. I have some funny stories about the way people in suits think imagination-filled children should learn math and science devoid of adventure.

Walter: OK I will. Goodnight Richard, thanks again.

On Halloween, Faraz, who lived at the end of the street, was walking with his children on their way home after trick-or-treating when a drunk driver struck him. He shattered the windshield and was thrown into a wall. His children, luckily, were unharmed. The accident left him unresponsive and more than a week passed before he began showing any signs of a positive recovery. The whole neighborhood helped his wife Dahlia with food delivery and errands. They all started a fundraiser to cover Faraz's medical expenses, and Richard helped watch the kids while Dahlia spent most nights at the hospital.

Death

Walter: Is Dahlia holding up OK?

Richard: I don't think so. I'm trying my best to not bring up anything related to Faraz and just help with whatever she needs. Mostly I walk the kids to school and pick them up while she's at work or the hospital.

Walter: I think that's probably best. I still can't believe all of this happened. It could have been any of us. It could have been our kids.

Richard: Yeah, tragic events like this bring up a lot of dark thoughts. This all brings me back to the summer of 2005.

Walter: That's when you lost Janice and your kids?

Richard: Yes. I returned to academia for a short stint in 2005 for a special summer lecture series at Stanford on the power of genetic programming and machine learning algorithms. The university offered to house me and my family for the summer in gorgeous Palo Alto. Lecturers were invited from around the world and we all converged in beautiful northern California to teach this incredible six week course to many adult learners.

Janice, James and Zoe all came with me for the summer. They had a blast. The kids only remembered a little about the west coast since we moved out before they were old enough to really enjoy its beauty. We spent time in all the parks, driving along the Pacific Coast Highway and just pretending to be Californians. It was a fantastic summer.

I needed to stay a few days longer since my lectures didn't match up perfectly with the start of their school year. They flew back a few days before me. I don't know if you remember the Rocky Mountain plane crash, but they were on that plane. The planes' navigation failed and the pilots couldn't find a place to land.

Walter: Oh my. I do remember that. I didn't realize it was more than 15 years ago.

Richard: Yeah it always feels like yesterday to me. Unfortunately and fortunately, death is the destination we all share. It's life's curse and greatest gift.

Walter: I guess so. But I would hardly call it a gift.

Richard: It is a gift. Death is the best motivator we have to live a full life and make the most of every day. You never know when we could be in Faraz's situation.

Walter: You're right, this whole event has really shaken me to the core. I don't think I ever really felt so fragile.

Richard: It sounds harsh, but death also helps clear out the old and make way for the new. It's the premature deaths that jar us because they feel so unnatural and unfair. The deaths that surprise us, make us realize our own mortality.

Thinking about death really helped me. I began to acknowledge the very finite and unpredictable amount of time I had left. Ever since I lost my family I've been hyperaware of the present and the uncertainty of my future. That's what I mean when I say it is a gift. I wasted so many moments before my family's death. Now, I live like I could die at any second. Not a day goes by that I don't think about my own timeline.

Walter: It's a shame we need something so tragic to help put life in perspective.

Richard: My family's death is an event that both exists and doesn't exist. When I think about them, they become real. And when I think about something else, they are distant memories. They lived a wonderful life with me. Now I live a wonderful life without them. Of course if I knew that they would be on a plane that would crash I would have never let them go. But this is the exact thing that can happen when we do anything. All paths are possible at the beginning and all converge to one outcome at the end.

Walter: Have you heard any good news about Faraz's condition?

Richard: It sounds like he's following commands now and might be getting off the ventilator. It's going to be a long road for him and his family.

Walter: I'm really glad our fundraiser has been so successful. I'm going to get the money to Dahlia tomorrow.

Richard: I think that will help a lot. I'm going to go pick up the kids from school. Talk to you later.

Walter: Later.

After spending close to two months in the hospital and another month at a rehab facility, Faraz was ready to return home. He made an incredible recovery with almost all function restored to his legs after many surgeries. Richard and Walter were almost finished with the portable wheelchair ramp they built to fit over the stairs at the Shahs' house when they got word that he was being released and would be home the next day. After Walter returned from work, they both hurried over to the Shahs' for final installation.

Conversation

Richard: So how did you get so good with construction?

Walter: I wouldn't call building this ramp construction, more like a small project. My dad was very handy and I guess I just learned while helping him do home improvement projects.

Richard: It's impressive. I would have put a board down and been done with it, but by building the ramp to fit into each step you've created amazing stability. Faraz is going to be impressed.

Walter: Yeah, this turned out better than I expected. They can just remove it when he no longer needs his wheelchair.

Richard: I don't think you needed my help at all.

Walter: Of course I did. Who would have held my tools.

Richard: Very funny.

Walter: Have you watched the news recently? See all this drama with the President and impeachment?

Richard: Nope. Haven't watched or read the news in at least 20 years.

Walter: Why am I not surprised. I know the news is dumb most of the time, but it's still good to be informed. Also, nice to have a few current event conversation starters.

Richard: I guess so, but there are so many more important things that could be talked about. Imagine meeting a new coworker and instead of saying "Good morning, have you seen the craziness of the impeachment?" you ask, "What part of town did you decide to settle into?" We spend so much time talking about things that don't matter and we almost never get to know people. You and I have had so many meaningful conversations that I actually understand or at least think I understand you.

Walter: I don't disagree. I think that's why sports are such a common talking point. It creates an immediate common interest without having to dig too deep.

Richard: Most people don't actually know anything meaningful about their friends. They enjoy each other's time because they have a few interests in common and that common interest keeps the peace. They talk about things like sports and movies, but know nothing about each other's true hopes and dreams.

Walter: You think people are just playing it safe? Do you think they realize they don't know anything meaningful about their friends?

Richard: Probably a combination of both. If you ask important questions to a friend there's a chance that the friend might ask important questions back. It's scary to be challenged.

Walter: Especially if those conversations expose cracks in the friendship.

Richard: True, but there's probably a better chance the conversation deepens the friendship. I only have a few really close friends, many of which I haven't seen in a very long time. We talk on the phone a few times a year and that's enough because we talk about life events and ideas that are meaningful.

Walter: Do you remember one of the first conversations we had?

Richard: Of course, you basically accused me of being a selfish old man by keeping my phone off.

Walter: I did not! I apologized for coming off so strong.

Richard: I know. I'm just kidding. We both started off pretty intense. But it set the stage for being great neighbors and friends.

Walter: We're lucky to live next door to each other. Most friends don't even do phone calls. They only chat using social media.

Richard: And that's one of the greatest reasons for modern loneliness. Social media is like living in NYC. Surrounded by people but completely alone. Living vicariously through observing the experiences of others but never connecting through deep conversation.

Walter: Well now that the ramp is done, would you want to pick up a few Italian dishes at Franco's deli and come over for dinner.

Richard: Sounds good. I might need to leave early. I have an interview tonight with an old colleague at 7 o'clock.

Walter: For what?

Richard: It's a video interview on using encryption to protect whistleblowers. It's for an educational series put on by the Human Rights Foundation

Walter: Sounds great. My kids need to start bedtime routines by 7:00 anyway so I'm sure we'll be finished before your interview starts.

For the first time in 5 years since Richard moved in, he wasn't on the front porch as Walter passed by on his way to work. He thought he recalled Richard mentioning an upcoming trip, but he had been too busy to remember to ask where or when. Slightly worried, he peeked through the windows in front and back just to make sure nothing inside looked amiss. There was no sign of him and his hatchback wasn't in the driveway so he must have traveled somewhere. Then after three weeks, Richard was back.

Traveling

Walter: Good to see you. Where have you been? I was a little worried.

Richard: Just returned from Japan. Didn't you get the note I put in your mailbox.

Walter: Oh no, I never saw it. I even investigated around your house just to check to make sure you weren't hurt and laying inside.

Richard: Sorry, I should have sent you a text.

Walter: So where'd you go?

Richard: I finally got the chance to see the Tsukiji Fish Market and explore Tokyo. It was a spur of the moment trip —plane tickets were ridiculously inexpensive.

Walter: How was it? Is it as awesome as videos make it seem?

Richard: Even better than I imagined. Tokyo was also really interesting. I could have spent months there and still felt confused. The degree of relativity was unbelievable.

Walter: Relativity?

Richard: Oh I must sound crazy. Sorry, Janice and I used to joke that the only reason to travel was for the relativity, otherwise, we might as well stay home. The more different the place the more reason to travel.

Walter: That's clever. I get it. Travel to places that are very different relative to your surroundings. If you live in Japan that fish market is pretty normal.

Richard: Yes, absolutely. When I'm in a different location I see myself relative to the new environment. In Japan, I feel like a slob and a fat giant in comparison to my surroundings. I talk fast here but slow there. I'm smart here and lost there. Any place I go with sufficient differences, helps provide a new understanding of my self relative to my surroundings.

Walter: Most people probably don't realize but I think that's a pretty universal feeling. We love to travel because of the newness.

Richard: I don't travel for the newness. I look for different. If I wanted new I could just travel to a new part of San Diego. People are really seeking a different perspective even if they think they just want something new. A different location provides an alternative perception of self relative to the surroundings. It feels new and exciting because we're a little uncomfortable. Since our identity isn't fixed, and it's defined in relation to the people and things around us, a new location helps us see ourselves differently.

Are you tall? Yes in relation to someone who is short. Are you loud, yes in relation to someone who is quiet. Are you adventurous. No, in relation to an experienced rock climber or global explorer. You are in relation to others. You are in relation to your past self.

Walter: And when you return home, does this new awareness stick for a while or do you drift back into your old ways? If you're like me, the busyness of life causes a quick reversion.

Richard: Yes I also revert back to normal. I don't really need the perception difference to stick because I need to return to normal and attend to things that are unique to my home. Just the fact that I felt differently in a new place is enough to make me aware of who I am when I'm at home.

Walter: Well I'm gad you're back and safe. Do you have any pictures of the trip.

Richard: No, I left my phone in the hotel when walking around.

Walter: Ha! Of course.

The city of San Diego, still in deep financial trouble, was about to cancel the building of a new natural history museum. An anonymous donation from an offshore corporation suddenly appeared at the front desk of the temporarily closed museum. The only stipulation attached to the check was that Richard Feinburg speak at the opening. Before cashing the check, the museum governing organization reached out to Richard. At first he declined to speak but after thinking about the situation more, he agreed to talk on a topic of his choosing. Thrilled, the museum agreed and construction was finished, allowing opening day to correspond with the first day of summer.

Free Will

Richard: Hey Walter, I'm giving a lecture at the opening of the museum of natural history tonight. Some deep pocketed rich person made a donation and stipulated that I speak at the museum. I have a free ticket for you and Chloe. If you can come, bring Cody and Mia, there's a whole kids area they can play in during my talk.

Walter: Wait a minute? Someone is forcing you to talk?

Richard: No, not really forcing, I agreed to speak, but the museum said that they received a donation contingent on me being present at opening day. The donor gave enough money to finish construction and fund the museum for 3 years.

Walter: Do you know who would do that?

Richard: No idea. I really don't know anyone here in San Diego except you and some surfing buddies. Of course I know a lot of very rich entrepreneurs but after asking my friends and former colleagues I have no idea who would do such a crazy thing. I initially thought it was an old friend pulling a practical joke. It's all very strange. Anyway, I agreed to talk and am happy to help out the museum.

Walter: What are you talking about tonight?

Richard: Apparently I can talk about anything I want. I figured I could use some practice talking about free will. It's one of the ideas I've been trying to write up as a blog post.

Walter: You're writing about free will?

Richard: Actually the myth of free will. But the museum doesn't know that yet.

Walter: Is this going to cause a lot of controversy?

Richard: No more than I usually create.

Walter: OK, I'll see if we can go tonight. Can you make your case against free will for me in five minutes just in case I can't attend?

Richard: I think so. Do you control your own thoughts?

Walter: Yes.

Richard: Do you agree that if you didn't control your own thoughts it would be hard to believe in the idea of free will?

Walter: Yes I agree.

Richard: Do you agree that we have a subconscious?

Walter: Yes

Richard: By definition, subconscious thoughts are outside of our control. For example, one day you might not be able to remember a person's name and then randomly a week later that name pops into your thoughts. You can't remember your best friend's birthday and then a day later without even thinking about it, you suddenly remember it. We have uncontrollable subconscious thoughts that randomly bubble up into conscious awareness. Doesn't that imply that we don't have complete control over everything we think about?

Walter: Maybe.

Richard: OK, sit here on my step, close your eyes, and don't think about anything. As if you were meditating—just focus on breathing. Tell me after five minutes if you can control your thoughts. I'll be back, I need to use the bathroom.

five minutes later

Richard: OK I'm back.

Walter: I see what you mean. Just like when I had tried meditation, lots of random stuff entered my mind, but I don't see how that impacts my free will. I choose what I want to act on regardless of what appears in my mind.

Richard: Don't you think that those thoughts impact what you ultimately decide to do? The second your eyes close and you try to focus on one thing, you're flooded with thoughts outside of your control. Where is your free will in controlling those thoughts? Of course you can try and consciously silence them, but as soon as you try, more thoughts emerge.

Walter: But how do those subconscious events prove that my daily choices are not free? I can still consciously choose to do whatever I want. Even though all that stuff entered my mind. I still chose to sit on your step.

Richard: But would you have sat on the step if I didn't suggest it? The most important point is that conscious choice and free will are not the same thing. We are conscious and we make choices but those choices are not 100% free. We are influenced by many things outside of our control. This can be world events, local events, emotions, hunger, or just about anything you think of. We don't live in a vacuum and as you can see from your five minutes of meditation, we barely even control our own thoughts. Your choice to stay seated was influenced by my suggestion.

Walter: But I can still choose to act even if I'm influenced by people and events outside of my control.

Richard: Freedom implies complete autonomy. If many things outside of our control are influencing us, then we are not free. Take it one step further. There are things that we just can't bring ourselves to do because of our current and past mental states.

Try this experiment, just to humor me. Right now, try and stop loving your wife. If you were truly free to make any choice, you could stop loving her and then after this experiment go back to loving her.

Walter: OK point made. I can't do that.

Richard: See, you are not free. You can only act within a range of possibilities. Your ability to act is not only within the restraint of your current society but influenced by your brain chemistry. Specific imbalances can shift your mental disposition drastically whether towards depression, anxiety, or any emotional state.

Walter: So, if it isn't me making my own choices, then does this negate all responsibility?

Richard: No that is a common misunderstanding. You still have responsibility. We have the ability to do some things and not others. You don't mindlessly react to every thought that enters your mind. It's just that those choices are influenced by all of the other factors outside of your control. And then there are other choices you cannot make because of your life experiences. That's why you can't just decide to stop loving your wife.

We are neither free nor slave to subconscious or external influences. Just because we are hungry doesn't mean we eat the first thing that comes into view. But at the same time we don't really control when we are hungry. Our mind is deeply entangled with unknown and autonomic forces of the body and environment, so much that we are certainly not free.

Take it a step further. Are you free to stop liking your favorite foods? Were you free to choose your favorite foods in the first place? Absolutely not. You like to eat specific things because of your taste buds, memories of family dishes, sense of smell, and experiences during special holidays. Not to mention countless unknown factors.

So no only do we not control our subconscious thoughts which influence our consciousness but we don't even control why we have specific preferences, wants, desires, and fears. Yes, we can try and often successfully change ourselves but there is much that we cannot change. Plus there are events we cannot control that will change us in the future.

Walter: Interesting, if everyone understood this then we would probably be a lot more understanding of differences.

Richard: That's ultimately my point in discussing this topic. Understanding an individual's lack of free will should translate into a realization that everyone around you also lacks free will. We have personal responsibility but are also products of randomness.

Walter: And the most important question. Will there be food tonight?

Richard: I think so. I'll send you a message if the food looks bad so you can prepare for the kids.

Walter: Thanks.

Richard: And even if I don't see you tonight, let's go for a surf tomorrow morning if you're up for it.

Walter: Sounds good.

Richard's speech was well received. It was as if everyone realized they were in the matrix and their minds were not wholly their own. As he mingled with the museum directors, Richard asked who had requested his presence, but they seemed to know no more than he did. The anonymous donor remained a mystery. The kids didn't care about any of the philosophy of mind talk or the big donations, they just wanted to play. Cody and Mia had so much fun in the dinosaur-themed play area that everyone ended up having a late bedtime. Early morning surfing became late morning surfing.

Fear of Quitting

Richard: Did people enjoy my talk?

Walter: Yes absolutely. Judging by the conversations I overheard, people were very surprised.

Richard: Good. Practicing was really helpful for my upcoming essay. I'll probably be able to post on my site in the next few weeks. How's the new job at Tenex going?

Walter: Not as good as I hoped. I might end up quitting.

Richard: Oh no. What's the issue?

Walter: Well, the pay was always a problem but I thought I could get over it with the stock options and fun team. Turns out that Tenex as a company is really dysfunctional. All the problems were hidden from me when interviewing. There are some pretty loud personalities that clash a lot. The tech is awesome and the mission to help decentralize internet communication is still great, but the workplace negativity destroys morale and productivity.

Richard: If you quit, what would you do?

Walter: Well that's why I haven't quit. I actually don't know what I would do. Unfortunately I'm far from independently wealthy. At the same time, if I stick with the job, the stock payout could be huge.

Richard: Are you most afraid of losing the salary? I'm sure you can find a new job very easily. Few people have such expertise in distributed systems.

Walter: Yeah, I think that's what I am most afraid of. Cody is five years old and Mia is going to turn two soon, so I don't want to be without health insurance and a steady income. Not to mention that quitting just feels wrong. I've learned so much from working at this job despite the CTO's crazy personality.

Richard: Is it really the health insurance holding you back? Pay attention to your fears. What's the exact thing you are afraid of? What's the worst case scenario if you quit?

Walter: I'm not sure. I've never quit a job without a new one lined up.

Richard: I've realized that it isn't the actual worst case scenario we fear it's the unknown. If you spend time thinking through actual worst case scenarios you realize that most of them are not really as bad as imagined. It's the uncertainty that scares most. Once you plot out the actual scenario the problem demystifies and fear evaporates.

Walter: Well if I quit and don't find a job Chloe's income is not enough to keep us afloat. San Diego, while beautiful, isn't cheap.

Richard: Right, but you could wait until you have a new job lined up before quitting to make life easier. And regarding health insurance, many plans let you stay on board and pay for an extension after you leave your job. Before you fear the expensive health insurance, find out what it actually costs. What else are you afraid of?

Walter: Well I'm not really that afraid of finding a new job. I already know of a few great communication startups and have connections locally from friends.

Richard: OK so what's the worst case scenario?

Walter: That I anger my boss by quitting.

Richard: Who cares if he's angry at you for quitting in a nice way? That's absurd. You've worked for him and he paid you. You traded your time for money and there's no more obligation beyond that trade. They received your time in the form of product advancement and now it's time to part ways. Nothing more, nothing less. Do not fear something you have no control over.

Walter: And if quitting causes my boss to be concerned about trade secrets?

Richard: I had the same issue when I left a blue sky think-tank where everyone had signed piles of non-disclosures. I perseverated about leaving for months and was stressed out. My wife constantly criticized me about my indecision to leave because I was mostly worried about what my coworkers would think. I had an offer to star in the *History of Computing* TV series.

One day as she was goading me, she hit me with the question, "Why do you care what other people think?" I had no answer because I didn't really care about what others thought. I knew I needed to quit and pursue other things that would made me happy and reduce stress.

Again it wasn't the worst case that worried me. I was afraid of the unknown. I feared what people might think about my decision. I didn't need to be worried about anyone's opinions because I knew I would never leak anything from a nondisclosure. I also had no control over other's opinions so worrying about it did me no good. From that day forward I stopped worrying about what others thought and just did what I felt was right for myself and family.

Walter: For some reason, quitting still feels like failing, especially since I just started this job.

Richard: It shouldn't. Whenever you say no to an opportunity you say yes to future possibilities. There's a cost to every decision. Everything we spend time on means we don't spend time on other things. When you quit you're really saying yes to new options. Quitting early when situations are obviously wrong, allows for a quick transition to new and often better possibilities.

Walter: I like that philosophy. Quitting is really just changing course.

Richard: Of course, you're still going to work hard, just at something else. You're not ending your career, just changing projects.

After Walter quit his job, he had a month off before starting at telecommunication startup Orion. What he thought would be guaranteed relaxation, quickly became more work at home. He thought he could sit around and do whatever he wanted while unemployed but Chloe had different expectations. She wanted an uptick in domestic help since he had more time to assist. Cooking, cleaning, and childcare became his main jobs. After a few weeks of constant bickering, Chloe insisted Walter take a two day meditation retreat to clear his head and return ready to help with two kids. Begrudgingly he agreed.

Make it your own

Richard: Hi Walter, I haven't seen you in awhile. Where have you been?

Walter: Just returned from a silent retreat.

Richard: I'm impressed. They aren't easy. I'm glad I didn't discourage you from trying meditation. How was it?

Walter: Incredible. It was Chloe's idea and I didn't really have a choice if I wanted a happy marriage. Staying silent for 48 hours is harder than I thought. The time away and the fact that there's nothing to do but reflect helped me a lot.

Richard: I attended a transcendental retreat once where they taught mantra based meditation. It was super cheesy but I guess a lot of people swear by the method. I think if you're going to meditate, the simplicity of zen is best.

Walter: Yes they taught zen on this retreat.

Richard: What did you learn?

Walter: The quietness helped create an awareness of feelings I often suppressed. I never realized the power of recognizing a feeling as it occurs. Before, when meditating, I never got to that point. I never felt anything when alone in a quiet room. But on this silent retreat I had an overflow of emotions and nothing could distract me. I became aware of my baseline level of anxiety.

I know you're somewhat negative on meditation but I think this retreat convinced me of its utility.

Richard: Agreed. I have no issues with meditation, just that it isn't for me and I never made it a daily practice. In modern times, the popularized forms of meditation focus a little too much on the sitting part and not enough on the daily awareness part.

Walter: That's fair. Meditation isn't a silver bullet and can't exist in a vacuum.

Richard: No matter what form of meditation or daily practice you adopt, make it your own. Subscribing to someone else's technique or school of thought can be helpful. But if a personal variation works better, use the variation.

In my case, I had a little mission statement that I would repeat over and over to myself, especially when feeling burned out. I'd say to myself, "I'm good at it, I love it and they are paying me." It became my own personal mantra. At the transcendental retreat, I described my mantra to one of the leaders. She told me that the Japanese have a word similar to my mantra and encouraged me to use one word when meditating. Since my phrase was similar to the Japanese word *ikigai*, she wanted me to replace my mantra with it.

Supposedly in Japanese, *ikigai* means a combination of what you love, what you do well, what earns money, and what the world needs. So I followed her instructions and repeated the phrase over and over but it just felt empty. After leaving the retreat and trying to do transcendental meditation over the next few months, I never found that one word as powerful as my own little mantra. There's power in making a phrase or an idea your own.

Walter: After enough practice could you have adopted the new mantra and formed a daily meditation around it?

Richard: I'm not sure. Why should I even try? I had something that already worked as a way to calm my anxiety.

Walter: In your case it sounds like you were already very self aware. Imagine you weren't. Do you think someone else's teachings would have helped?

Richard: Maybe. But you need to want the technique to work. You need an emotional connection to the habit for long term commitment. With any life improving activity, the value comes mostly from a belief in success. It's almost like a placebo. You believe it can work, you see results, and therefore it must work. Since it works you do more of the activity and see more positive results.

Walter: You're saying belief in the practice carries all the value?

Richard: Not all of the value. You can't believe in a bad activity and expect good outcomes. But most of the good originating from a positive activity results from belief that encourages consistency and commitment. In my case I didn't believe in the transcendental meditation practice so it didn't work.

Now that you believe in the techniques taught on your retreat, you've started to make the practice your own. This increases the chances of success.

Think about your kids. If they never believe in what you teach them, they will never continue practicing a good habit unless you are there reminding them. If they don't believe in brushing their teeth they'll skip brushing. But if you can help them learn why brushing is important and get them to do it on their own, they'll brush regularly. They have to want to do what you teach them and believe it is good.

Emotions give habits their power. My silly little mantra, calms me down because it has worked before and I want it to keep working. Pure circular reasoning.

Walter: I see what you're saying, but I'm not sure I feel the need to make any changes to the techniques they taught.

Richard: I don't think you'll be able to avoid making changes. Especially if you meditate everyday. You'll start to make small tweaks.

Most people meditate because successful people recommend meditation, and everyone wants to be successful. The step most miss, involves taking ownership over the activity. If this emotional connection doesn't occur and the practice isn't personalized, then you'll be doing something simply because someone told you to do it. This makes commitment very hard. Without commitment, there is no consistency and without consistency there is no habit.

Walter: Thanks for this. I hope I'll be able to continue meditation each morning.

Richard: Well don't feel limited by the meditation techniques you've been taught. If it works better for you to walk and think, do that instead. It'll be far more effective than any meditation taught by a particular teacher or coach.

Richard's educational shows and books on computer science and physics made him a popular contact in many science fiction circles. A few writers leaned on him as a resource to improve their writings, since he distilled complex topics into fun analogies. At the same time Richard found that reading fiction, especially stories with a strong basis in scientific fact, helped him imagine the future and develop new ideas. Usually once a year he would spend some time with an author and help review the science in their book for accuracy.

You

Richard: Hey Walter, I've been working on a proofread of a great sci-fi novel you'd probably like.

Walter: Is it by anyone that I'd know?

Richard: I'm not sure. He's written a few other books. Have you heard of *Timeshift by* Damian Liu? That was his most famous.

Walter: Sorry, never heard of him. Are you writing a forward for it or just providing feedback?

Richard: Damian is a good friend and I help him with scientific proofreading on certain sections. I try and provide some guidance on all his hard science novels.

Walter: So what's it about?

Richard: The multiverse. Well, specifically quantum superposition.

Walter: You've lost me. What's that?

Richard: The concept is related to Schrödinger's cat thought experiment. It's a principle of quantum mechanics where multiple quantum states exist at the same time. Then when observed, collapse into one actuality.

Walter: Sorry. I've heard of Schrödinger's cat but can you give me the readers digest summary?

Richard: OK, the first thing to understand, although this sounds weird, is that a quantum particle can be in multiple locations within a set of probabilities at the same time.

Imagine a cat in a closed box with a geiger counter attached to poison. You cannot see inside. If the geiger counter detects a radioactive particle the poison is released inside the box. The cat is alive when you put it in the box. You then place the box next to a substance that emits radioactive particles.

Since particles at the quantum level exist probabilistically at many locations some particles emitted by the decaying radioactive atoms can exist inside and outside the box simultaneously. This means that the cat could be alive or dead at the same time.

The outcome is dependent on the location of the particles. But the particles' locations interact with themselves creating the superposition simultaneously in the box and out of the box. All we know is that the particles within a series of probabilities have a likelihood of being in a specific place at a specific time.

Although somewhat absurd, mathematically this means the cat is both alive and dead at the same time. When the box is opened the possibilities converge to one reality. Our observation of the experiment influences the outcome to a degree. You only know if the cat died when you open the box. If you keep the lid closed then multiple possibilities continue to exist.

Walter: I vaguely remember this from undergrad. Even the act of observing particles like an electron influences the electron. Right?

Richard: Essentially you're right. And if this superposition principle from the quantum scale is applied to the macro scale, you have the phenomenon known as the multiverse. There could be a large if not infinite number of universes just like ours each with slight differences. We can only know the one actualizing to our reality in our time-space. But over time with even slight differences, each universe slowly drifts apart and eventually diverges entirely. Differences compound differences.

Walter: And this novel is about the multiverse?

Richard: Specifically about a physicist who finds a way to traverse to other realities in the multiverse. Somewhat far fetched but with some fun science driving the plot.

The best part of the book is the question posed by the main character, "What makes you truly you?" He begins to see versions of himself in each parallel reality he visits and many behave exactly like him. In some realities, other versions have radically different personalities and beliefs.

Walter: What do you mean?

Richard: If there are multiple versions of you in different simultaneous universes each in parallel are they the same as the "you" in this universe? Each of the versions of you have slight variations of your experiences. At some point would enough small differences change you?

Walter: Are you asking me if I become different because of my choices?

Richard: At what point do you change because of the changes occurring around you? If the world radically changed, how long would it take for you to change as well? This goes back to our other conversations about the self. What influences your identity?

Walter: Yeah, again an impossible question to answer. You never really know a person's defining feature. So many events and experiences make us who we are.

Richard: Exactly. We are more a product of our reality than an individual creating our own reality. Just like an electron, we respond to being observed. Every interaction creates us. If you change enough of our environment we reach a tipping point and change as well. If circumstances were extreme for long enough, you could become an entirely different person.

Walter: I think memory plays a big part. If you change enough memories, the person profoundly changes. I saw this first hand with my grandmother who had Alzheimers. So much of her personality changed as her sense of self was lost along with her memory.

Richard: And memories are just a collection of experiences. Since experiences make up most of our identity, if you could change enough of a person's experiences in theory you could change the person.

In the multiverse, an endless number of possibilities are being actualized, creating variation after variation. Each fork in the road we choose, limits our future choices. With each choice our potential changes. Each choice we make removes possibilities and creates new possibilities as we collapse our existence into current reality.

Walter: Is this what you meant when you said that the future doesn't exist?

Richard: That's sort of an oversimplification but it gets to the essence of this book, which is why I like it so much. The future is just one of many possibilities.

Walter: Fascinating stuff. Do you think the multiverse actually exists?

Richard: I have no idea, but it seems plausible.

In the early '90s Richard starred in a TV show teaching science to kids. All of his colleagues joked that he was the new Mr. Rogers. For three years he was a household name and every kid requested his science kits for Christmas. Last year, Richard went back in the studio to help remaster and add new episodes to the historic program which was released online. The new version of the show starred a greying Richard interacting with the younger scientist version of himself.

Be a student not a guru

Walter: You'll never guess Cody's favorite show to watch.

Richard: What?

Walter: *The Professor and the Kids!* Especially the one where you teach the names of the planets.

Richard: I'm so glad he likes the show. I was a little nervous about appearing along side my younger self but they made me look good as a mad scientist. It's neat the way they have young me and current me in the same episodes.

Walter: Yes, it's really cool what they did with the two versions of you. Cody watched a lot of episodes as part of a summer space camp. I don't think he realizes it's you.

Richard: I've only watched two clips. I can't bring myself to listen to my voice so I shy away from personal media appearances.

Walter: Just curious, how have you kept up the energy to do so many educational science shows and lectures? I feel like you've done more TV than Neil deGrasse Tyson and Carl Sagan combined.

Richard: It might seem like I'm always doing shows but that's just the magic of video. Projects usually have a 6 month commitment, followed by many years off. During the time off, all of the recordings trickle out giving the appearance that I work nonstop.

Walter: You have to admit, you created a lot of content. I still find it amazing that you have time to teach science and work on so many open source projects at the same time.

Richard: It seems like I work a lot, but I take a lot of time off. I find that learning happens when I listen and reflect. Understanding happens when I teach. Without extended periods of time off from doing public teaching and lecturing I could never have found the time to work on difficult problems.

Walter: Is public speaking and educating fun?

Richard: Some of it is fun, but other times I teach to help solidify my own understanding of concepts I think I know well. I can get wrapped up in complex cutting edge science but forget how to explain the basics to a new learner. If I can't explain something to a child then I probably don't adequately understand what I think I know. Excessively complex topics often mean inadequate understanding. Concise and simple explanations are usually the most correct. As Einstein said, "Everything should be made as simple as possible, but not simpler."

At the same time, if I ever begin to feel like a know-it-all or a guru, I take time off to read, write, and immerse myself in a new area of study. If I spend too much time in a position of authority, then people treat me like I have all the answers and at some point I begin to think I know everything. As soon as I immerse myself in something new and feel like a student again I realize my ignorance.

Walter: Well I can't thank you enough. Your web shows inspired me to pursue a career in computer science. And it's such joy to see my son excited about space as a kindergartner.

Richard: Getting compliments like that makes it all worth while. Education helps elevate the value of the world. Surprisingly, few scientists want to educate the public. Most desire recognition for their discoveries and only focus on educating their colleagues. Plus, universities rarely reward educators, because they don't receive large grants. This was why I felt so compelled to leave traditional academia and teach independently.

In the early 2000s a site with anonymous owners appeared online. ScienceOpen.org offered a peer reviewed alternative to traditional platforms. Unlike other open platforms ScienceOpen published on all topics and encouraged studies with negative as well as positive findings. They charged no reprint fee, had no paywall, and no open access charges. The site asked for a recurring yearly donation of a dollar and encouraged preprint distribution of prior publications. Publishers attempted to shut the site down and created lawsuits claiming unauthorized redistribution of prior published works. The site through a series or proxies became impossible to stop. Ten years later after most publishers were economically bankrupt, the three founders revealed themselves during a small asset sale.

Money as a means

Walter: Congrats on the sale of ScienceOpen.org! I guess it was a long time coming for you. How did you manage to stay anonymous this whole time? Aren't you worried about legal recourse?

Richard: Oh, you read that Business Insider piece. It isn't really a sale. They somehow managed to get all the facts wrong. We haven't been anonymous for a while. A few reporters were kind enough to keep our identities private and many in the scientific community knew the operators. We just kept a low profile as owners.

Walter: So you still manage the site?

Richard: No, I am getting too old. I started the project almost 20 years ago when I was in my 50s after years of frustration with publishing papers.

Walter: So who runs it now?

Richard: The site mostly runs itself with help from thousands of volunteers. The other two co-founders, Dipesh and Jaime, do routine site maintenance. Our code has essentially ossified and is fully open source so anyone can replicate the site if it stops working. I sold my shares to them and they sold it to a non-profit. We had an odd contract that states we can only sell our shares to each other and if two people have a majority ownership, then

51% of total shares must be transferred to a nonprofit holding company.

Walter: So you don't want the company to ever grow bigger?

Richard: The site's original goal has exceeded my wildest dreams. All I ever wanted was a place where researchers could publish their work for free and have it peer reviewed and available without a paywall. I want such a place to exist for as long as it still has an engaged user base.

Walter: And it was sustainable with the $1 a month membership?

Richard: Of course! It was profitable after 3 months. Think about the cost of publishing a scholarly article. How expensive is it?

Walter: I guess if you aren't printing a journal, hosting pdf files is pretty cheap.

Richard: Exactly. I don't pay for the research, I don't pay for peer reviewers. I barely pay for hosting costs. All that's required is a $1 yearly membership. If you can't afford the membership, you submit a request and we grant temporary 6 month access to everything, no questions asked.

Walter: So why didn't everyone just request temporary access?

Richard: Because we were so good to our customers. We served researchers better than any journal. ScienceOpen stood in stark contrast to all other publishers that either charge an open access publishing fee, or fund their publication with pharmaceutical ads and paywalls. We let members read everything and we kept membership dirt cheap and never raised the price. People want to support businesses that honestly provide value to customers.

Walter: Why didn't other publishers just lower their prices and adopt a similar model?

Richard: Because they exist with the end goal of making money. Like most businesses, science journals value money as the end not the means. For most journals, although they don't come out and say it, the science is a means for them to keep accumulating as much money and power as possible.

Walter: And you guys didn't need the money?

Richard: It was never a primary source of income for us. But more importantly we all viewed the money as a means to run a sustainable business. We used money paid to us by the customer to improve the lives of our customers. Sure we made money but we only made money so that we would could keep our customers happy. Without external shareholders or venture capitalists we didn't need to answer to anyone but our customers.

We built a business with the goal of helping the people who paid us money. We worked only for that end. We needed money like all businesses do but we never prioritized earnings growth. We just wanted sustainability and longevity. If you keep expenses low, then you can keep charges low and you can make customers even happier.

Walter: So I guess you never took funding because of the nature of the business. Tough to remain anonymous if someone knows who to pay when buying a stake in the company.

Richard: Yes that is true. But in reality, the second you take funding for a business you work for someone else, not your customer. You work for the venture capitalists or the shareholders. We required a paying customer to give us the means to serve them. Without a paying subscriber we had no way of achieving our goal of democratizing publishing. This directly aligned our mission with the subscribers' needs. Subscribers allowed our growth to be 100% organic. If we didn't get more customers we didn't grow. This would have been a signal that maybe our idea was not as good as we thought.

Walter: And in the process you bankrupted almost every major publisher.

Richard: Well that wasn't the intended goal but it certainly helped prove to the world that people disliked traditional publishing.

If the public funds research, then the public should have inexpensive and quick access to the results. Most large high impact research is funded by the taxpayer. It makes no sense to put barriers like paywalls between the funder and the study results.

Walter: So why sell your stake? Couldn't the mission be corrupted by the other owners who might decide that they now want to get rich?

Richard: I suppose it could, but at this point, we have forever changed how independent researchers access scientific results. Even if ScienceOpen goes away or becomes corrupted, the idea of universally and freely available research is so ubiquitous that another site would just take our place.

Ideas are more infectious than any virus. Our idea has now infected the minds of every young scientist. Our idea has changed culture. Most scientists don't even think of submitting their paper to a private journal.

Walter: And you don't care at this point if someone takes your place as the most popular scientific publisher?

Richard: If someone takes our place I would be thrilled. It means that someone else advanced our mission and serves the researcher better than us.

We never really cared about protecting our business from disruption. We used our business to solve a problem and if the problem is solved and our businesses is no longer needed then it's a victory for the world.

Walter's position at Orion cast him into the spotlight when a major power outage in southern California left entire cities in the dark. All internet and cellular communication was also down. The National Guard set up emergency supply stations as people panicked. Until power was restored no cellular towers worked. Internet communications were down from Los Angeles to San Diego. Orion distributed small solar-powered mesh repeaters to the community, allowing users with their app to talk over the distributed internet relay. The peer to peer network spanned all the way north to the Santa Ynez Valley where electricity was still stable. Users in San Diego could send text messages nationwide and have them transmitted via the last hop in Santa Barbara, where the mesh connected to an active internet connection.

Surprise People

Richard: Your little startup has really saved the day! People can't stop talking about this incredible mesh network you guys created. I sent a message to my cousin in Baltimore using your relay. Really great stuff.

Walter: We've been grateful for all the community support. Even the National Guard connected a relay endpoint to their satellite uplink. Now the hops don't need to go all the way to Santa Barbara.

Richard: Incredibly impressive engineering, the repeaters are really robust.

Walter: Yeah. I'm just glad our app withstood this stress test. I feel a little guilty that this terrible event has been so positive for our company.

Richard: And Chloe told me that you're giving a talk at Google next week.

Walter: Yeah, I'm nervous and excited. It's a small talk but still very cool. Any tips or advice for giving a technical presentation?

Richard: People learn when surprised. The emotional spark that occurs when a new idea enters the listeners' mind is momentous. People know this and want to listen to presentations that surprise. The best talks leave the audience intrigued and curious enough to investigate further. You need to surprise the audience at the beginning to draw them in immediately.

Walter: Surprise them with something new or just an interesting way of looking at an old problem?

Richard: Both if you can. You'll be tempted to give an introduction of yourself or speak for a few minutes on background and context. Don't do that. Assume they know who you are and what your company does. Keep the content short and concise, keep it intriguing and only present things that are new. No one wants to hear a talk on a subject they already know, they want to hear novel ideas. And they want to know immediately if your talk is interesting, so don't wait until the end to surprise them.

Walter: OK, good advice. I was going to give a small overview of our company. I guess that's silly since they invited me.

Richard: Exactly. Let them ask you about Orion if they want to know more. Get right to the exciting points and keep them on the edge of their seats.

You'll be tempted to fill the whole time slot. Try and only take a third of the time. This will force you to be concise and only present new and surprising ideas. There will be time for people to ask questions that expand upon the areas of interest.

Walter: I'm not sure my talk will be that profound. I'm really just describing the power of mesh networks.

Richard: I guarantee there's something novel that you do with your meshing or a difficult problem you've solved that will be of interest. Present on that. Your audience already knows the power of mesh networks. They invited you to tell them what they don't know. I guarantee they want to know how you achieved such stability with the current deployment.

Walter: I like that tip on keeping it short. I should time myself going through the talk before I add any more slides.

Richard: Oh slides are the worst! Get rid of as many slides as you can. You are there to entertain with novelty. If you can do the presentation with 5 slides, it will be exponentially better than one click every minute.

Walter: OK thanks for the advice. Here, this is for you. It's a new prototype of our mesh base station so you can serve as an uplink when we get power fully restored.

Richard: Fantastic. I can actually hook it up now with some solar panels and an old iridium phone I just reactivated.

A few weeks later, Walter awoke to ambulance lights on the street. Richard, drenched in sweat, was sitting upright in a stretcher clutching his chest while the paramedics wheeled him down the sidewalk. They were frantically strapping an oxygen mask to his face, while reading the flashing indicators on their monitor. Walter was just able to run outside and ask about the hospital destination before the paramedic team left. Tempted to follow the ambulance, Walter, instead made sure Richard's house was locked up and then unsuccessfully tried to sleep. The next morning, the Carlisles visited Richard at the Scripps ICU.

Who remembers us

Walter: Hi Richard, I'm sorry I didn't get here earlier, I figured the whole family would want to come. Mobilizing everyone took longer than expected. I wanted to be here first thing in the morning.

Richard: Don't apologize. Unless you could place a cardiac stent and repair a coronary aneurysm, getting here earlier would have done nothing. I only needed the cardiologist and cardiothoracic surgeon, who were waiting for me. Getting here early would have created extra stress on your end. I'm glad you're here now.

Walter: How do you feel?

Richard: Terrible. It's really hard to breathe if I don't sit straight up in bed and it's uncomfortable sleeping upright. Excuse my voice. I need to take breaks after talking.

Walter: What happened?

Richard: The doc said I suffered a large heart attack and the interventionist had difficulty stenting across the blockage. The amount of infarct has left me with an extremely poor ejection fraction. I'm not exactly a spring chicken, so a bypass is out of the question. The cardiologists recommended an external heart pump called an LVAD that I would wear. But even that isn't guaranteed success and they seem to hint that my chances of getting through the surgery are bad. I don't want that type of life and without the LVAD I'll never make it to a heart transplant.

Walter: Sorry, please excuse me. I swore I wouldn't cry. It's just tough to see you like this. What are your chances of recovery?

Richard: There are no chances. It's like the saying: "On a long enough timeline, the survival of everyone drops to zero." Times like these cast light on the simplicity of the world. We start, we live, and eventually, we end.

Walter: Don't say that. At least you made it through the procedure last night.

Richard: Yes it's good to be able to sit here and talk, but after my conversation this morning with the cardiologist I know that I'll never leave this hospital alive. I need all of these vasopressors just to keep a baseline blood pressure. The morning team was surprised how well I could talk and interact. I know the condition is bad when the doctors are surprised I'm not on a ventilator. I cannot live like this. I've just completed the DNR paperwork. I've asked them to withdrawal blood pressure support this afternoon.

Walter: Oh no. How can I help? Would you want me to try and reach out to your extended family?

Richard: No need. All of my close friends and family received a message from me this morning. Remember how I told you I was always writing my autobiography?

Walter: Yes.

Richard: Today everyone I know has been told of my condition and given a copy of my life's story. When you check your email, your copy will be there as well.

Walter: You're so matter of fact about all of this. I hadn't expected this at all. It's so hard for me to talk about your life as if it's about to end.

Richard: It is about to end, but that's OK. Please don't spend too much time here. You've been a wonderful person to know, if even for such a short period of time. Please, Walter, remember that in the end we live as long as someone has us in memory. When the last person dies who remembers us, we die with them.

Many people will remember me after I die because of what I've done. I'm going to keep living for a long time even though I won't be aware of it. I gave myself to others, and in return I remain in memory for a long time. Please do the same, at least with your family. It will bring you profound peace when it's your turn to die.

I couldn't have asked for a better friend these last few years. You're a wonderful father and an incredibly thoughtful person. My only regret is that we didn't get to go surfing more often. Please don't let Cody and Mia see me like this. Let them remember me as they do from the science videos they watch and their memories of us talking in your front lawn. Now give me a hug and let's say goodbye.

Walter: But you have no family here? Why don't I stay, at least until this evening. You shouldn't be alone.

Richard: OK, that would be nice.

Walter: Let me tell Chloe and I'll be back in a half hour. She's with the kids downstairs.

Richard: OK, don't be long.

With those final words, Walter let Richard sleep and walked out of the the ICU. He had such a hard time holding back his tears that he had to spend an extra moment in the hallway before rejoining his family in the hospital cafeteria. The children were already causing chaos and Chloe was pleased to see Walter return. As she saw the graveness of the situation in Walter's eyes, she fumbled for a pack of tissues in her purse.

Chloe: How is he? Should we all go up to visit now that the kids got some food?

Walter: He's not good. He doesn't really want the kids to see him so sick. But if you want to go up and say hi I can stay with the kids.

Chloe: OK, I understand.

Walter: It sounds like he doesn't have much time left. He's made peace with death and already asked the doctors to withdraw care. Will you be OK with the kids at home if I stay at the hospital for a few hours? I don't want him to be alone. I can just hail a car to take me home in the evening.

Chloe: Yes we'll be fine. Take as much time as you need. Send him my best, I'd go up and see him, but you know how uncomfortable I feel in ICUs.

Walter: I know, it's OK. I'll let him know you'd be up to see him if circumstances were different.

Walter said goodbye to the kids, who seemed to not mind heading home without seeing Richard. Then, he headed back to the ICU. As he got off the elevator he saw a code team run into Richard's room. He knew what was happening. This exact scene had played out with Chloe's mom when they were first married. He was too late. As he sat down on the nearest bench, he caught the eye of a nurse leaving the main hallway and stood up to ask if Richard had died. She just shook her head in the affirmative. Tears filled his eyes as time stopped. He couldn't remember if he had even said goodbye. He must have stared at the floor for over an hour because a chaplain sat next to him to make sure he was OK. Eventually the chaplain, aware of Walter's unwillingness to talk, just walked away. To anchor back to reality, he reached for his phone.

As he felt into his pocket, the phone lit up to indicate one new email notification: from Richard Feinburg - The Simple World. Slowly he tapped the message and began to read as tears erupted.

The Simple World

Hello Friends and Family,

I am dictating this message to my nurse as I lie in a hospital bed here in San Diego. He's been kind enough to type my email since I barely have enough strength to speak in full sentences. I've suffered a terrible heart attack and have no chance of living outside a hospital. It saddens me to share my last words by email and not in person.

Almost everyday, I wrote small pieces of my autobiography. It is attached below. Writing my story served as a journal of grief during my darkest moment when I lost my entire family. It helped keep my pride and ego in check during periods of fame. When I was overly zealous, writing my tale helped me revert to the mean. It helped put accomplishments and accolades in perspective. Most importantly, I wrote this so you would remember me.

When I recount my life's events, emotions, and expectations, each one matters very little. Taken together they meld and form my life. As a life, I also matter very little. When I die, the world continues as if I never existed. The universe continues to expand regardless of my extinction. The people I have taught and influenced collectively matter a little more. The passion for learning that they teach their circle of contacts creates even more influence. Larger and larger, the magnitude increases.

The world is simple, but understanding it is difficult. We often make it unnecessarily complex. Many phenomena can be distilled into exquisite equations and predicted with great accuracy, yet the human condition remains a mystery. Each of us has insight and data on one human experiment, our life. And when the experiment finishes, we do not have another chance to modify the variables.

But our output if timed correctly, can serve as the fuel for another fire. We can feed others' excitements and passions, or we can impede their progress. Whichever path we choose, or accidentally pursue, creates ripples that impact the other ripples in the pond of life. Focus on your local connections and everything else will naturally follow. I miss you all.

Live well,

Richard Feinburg

[attachment: richard-feinburg.pdf]

www.ingramcontent.com/pod-product-compliance
Lightning Source LLC
LaVergne TN
LVHW010100110826
845155LV00028B/426

* 9 7 8 1 9 4 9 5 1 0 2 4 9 *